This Tracing and Coloring book belongs to:

This handwriting book is designed for preschool and kindergarten kids learning the alphabet and beginning to write.

It contains letters and numbers to trace, with examples on each page of finished letters and numbers and then progressions with arrows to follow first, then lines to trace and finally empty lines to write in at the end of the section. Each page has a picture to color in to make the workbook more interesting and fun.

We suggest adult guidance initially, dependent on the age of the child and their stage of learning.

Read out the alphabet and trace each letter.

Section I:

Trace the letters and color in the pictures.

 is for Alligator

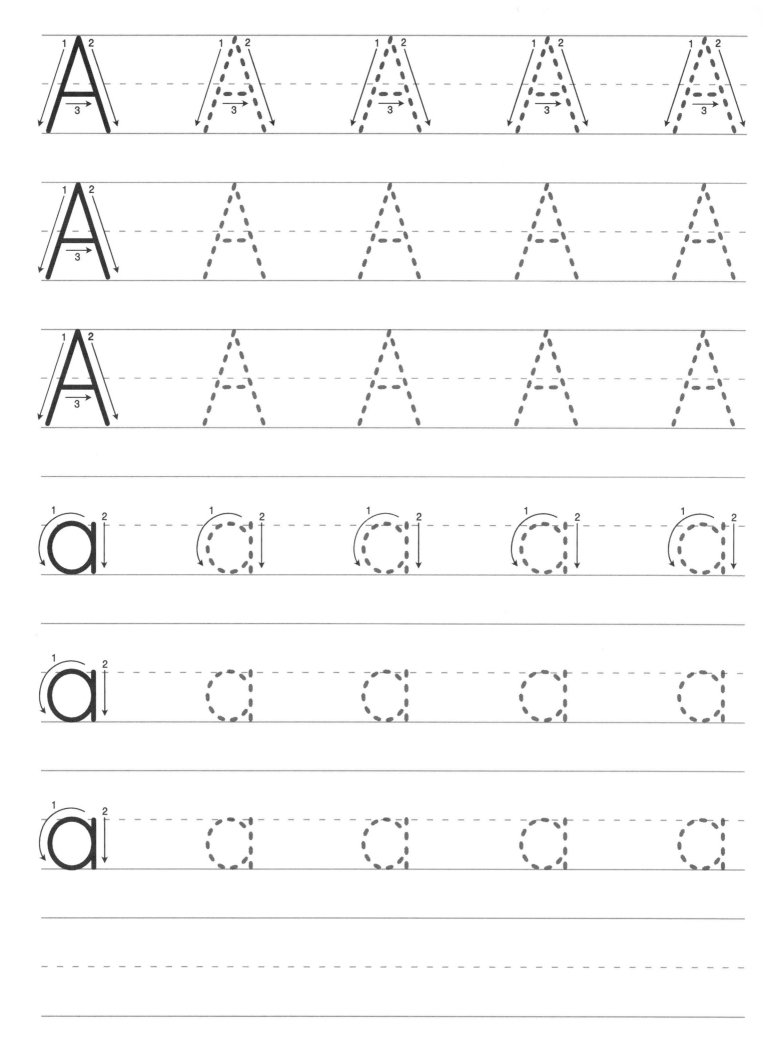

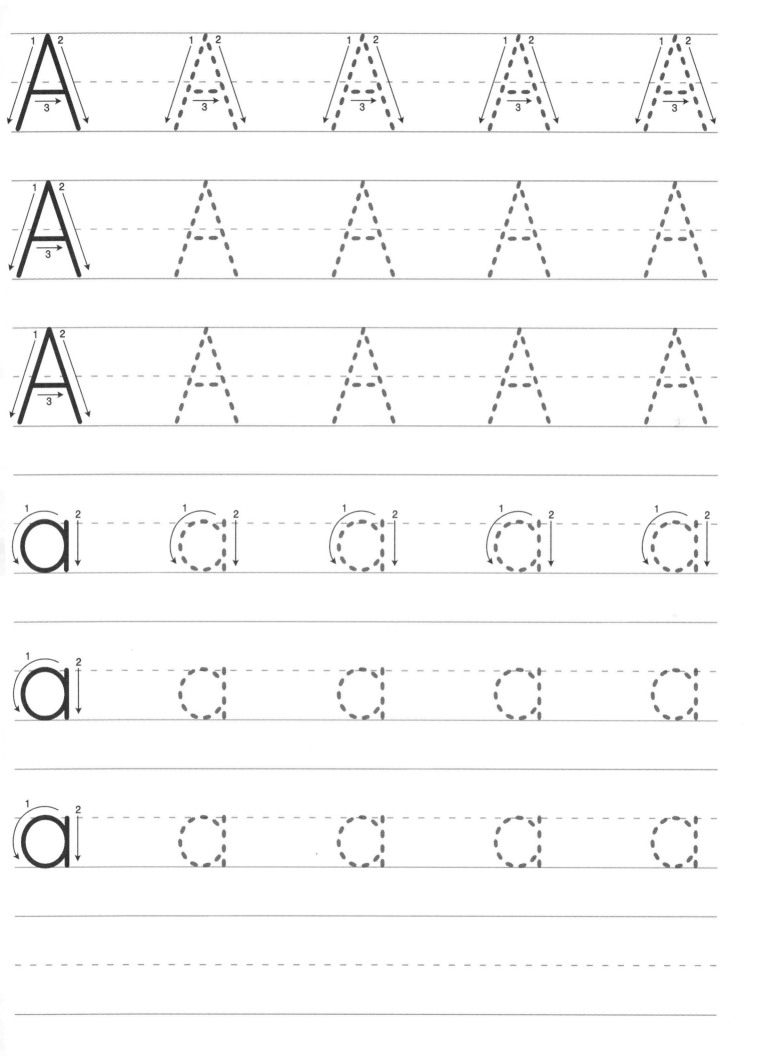

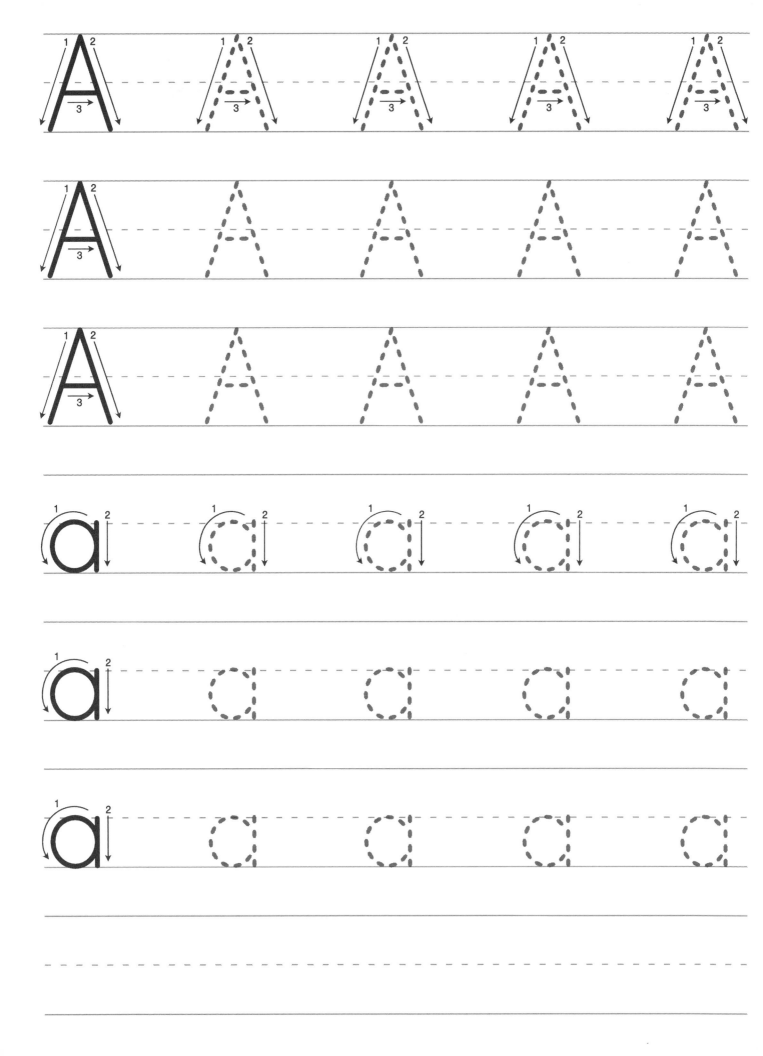

B is for Beetle

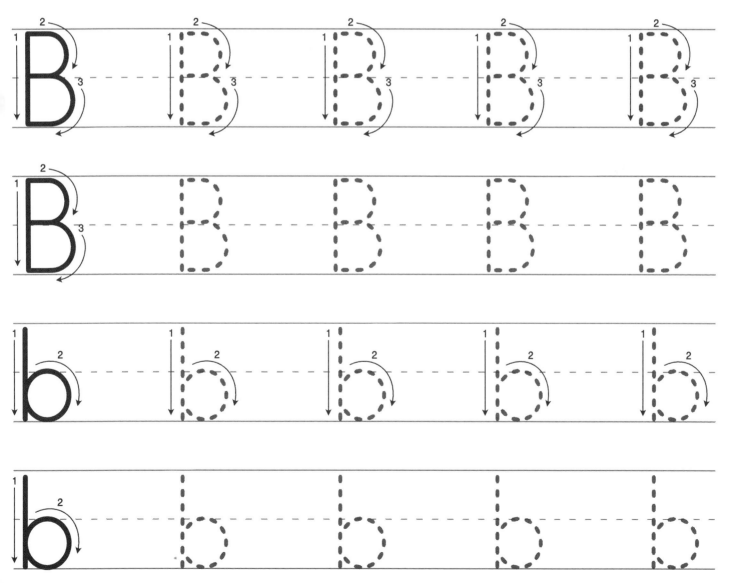

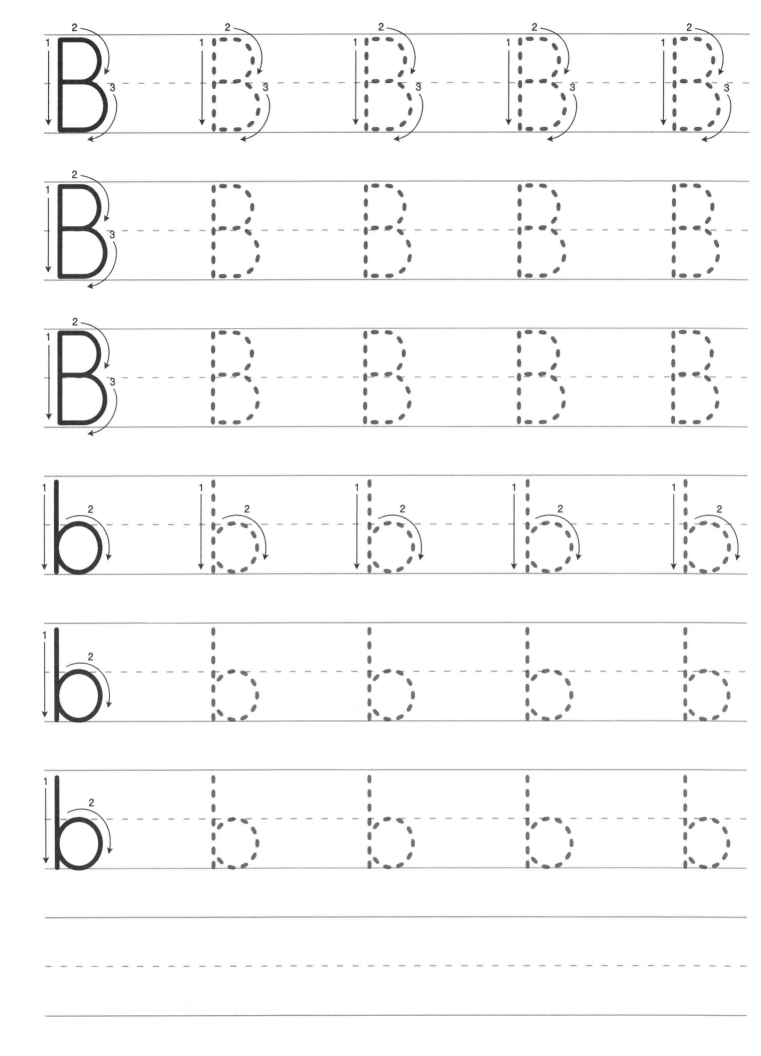

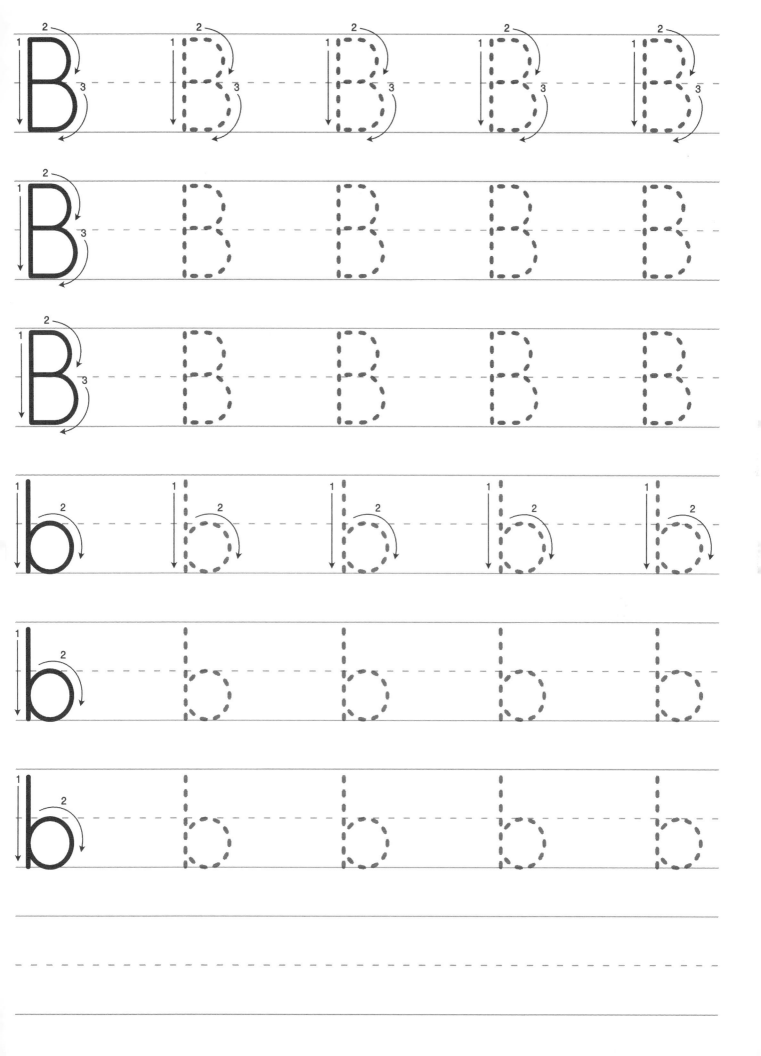

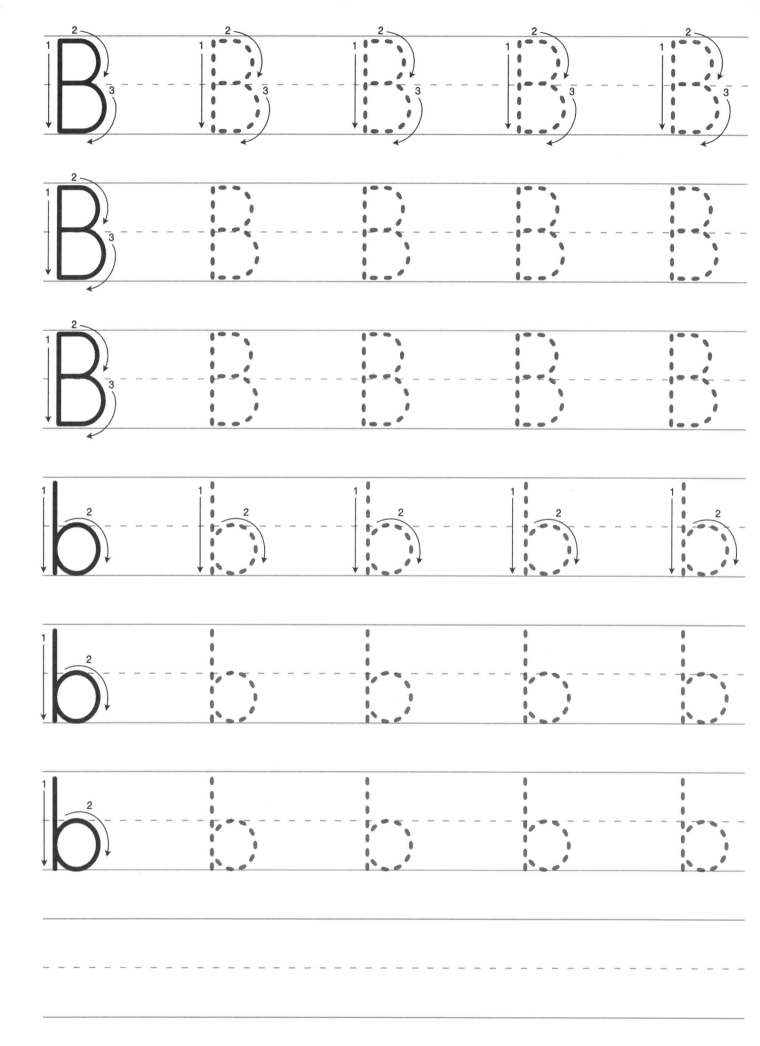

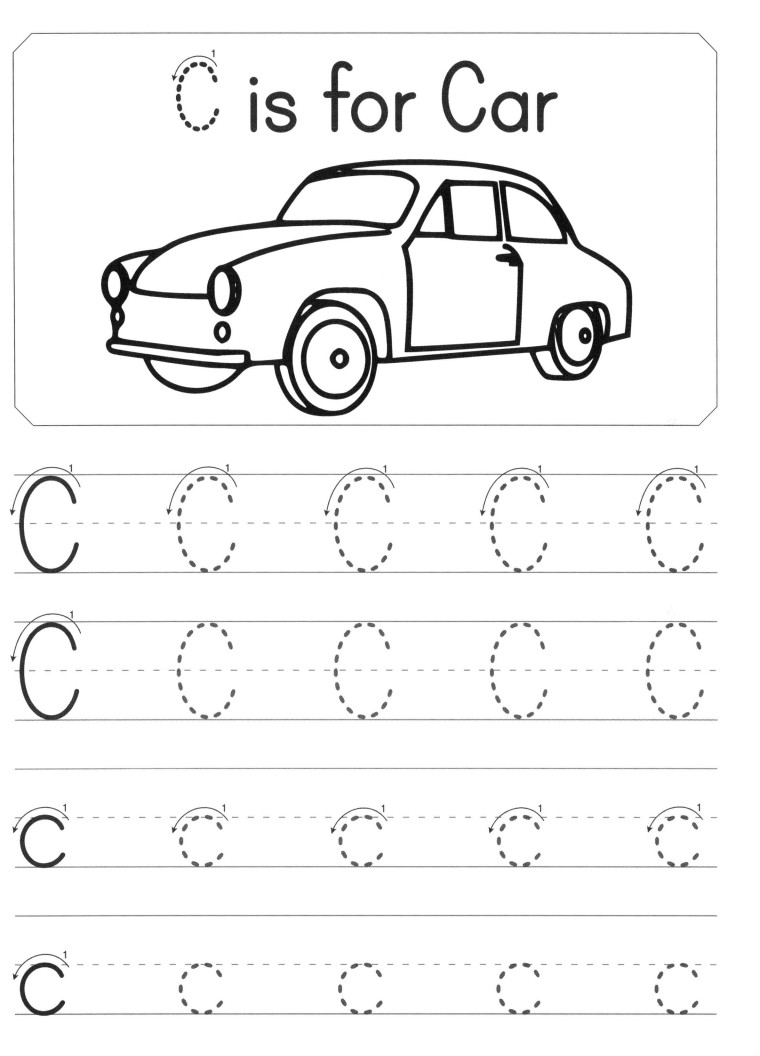

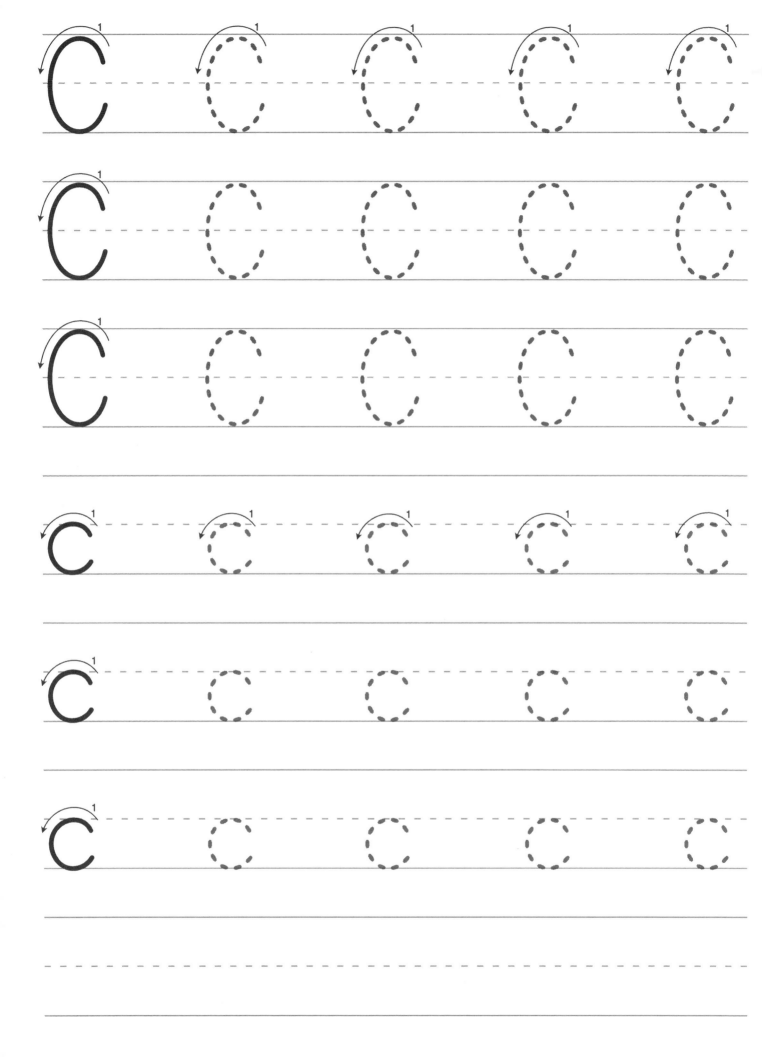

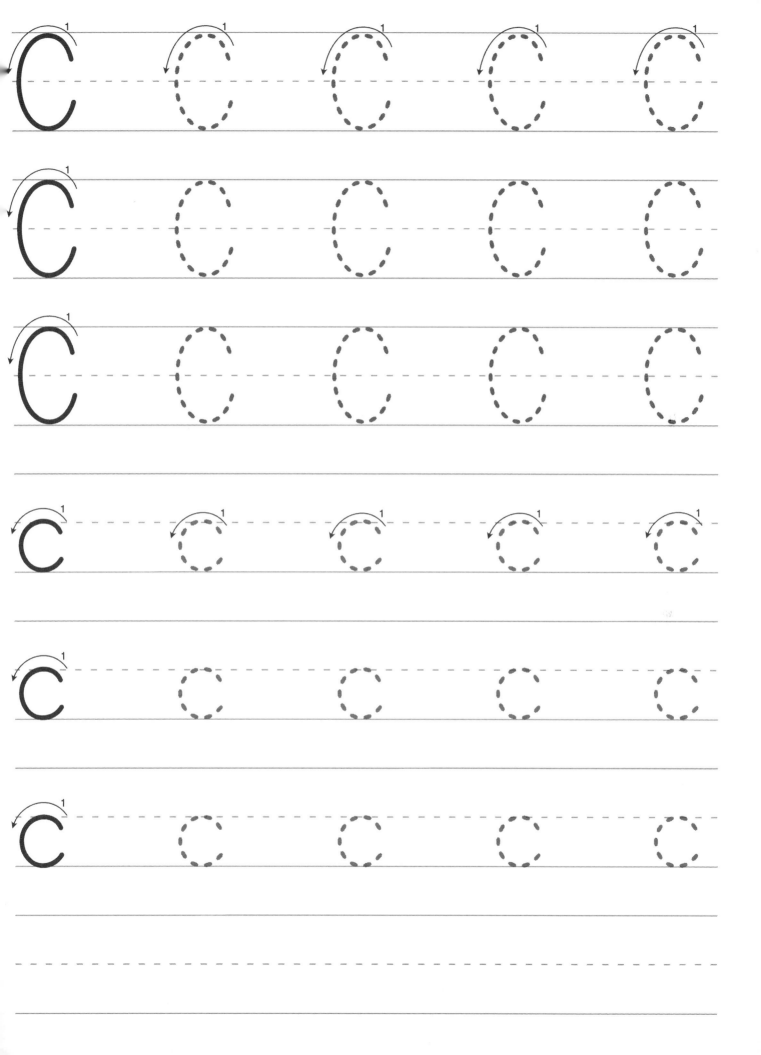

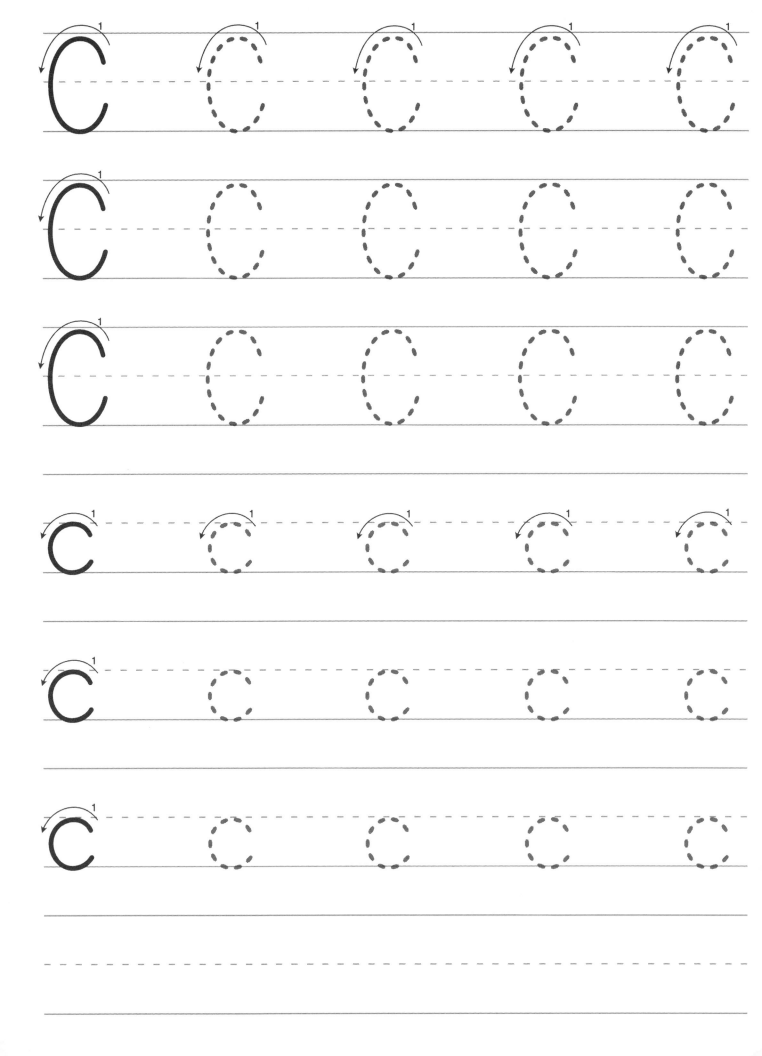

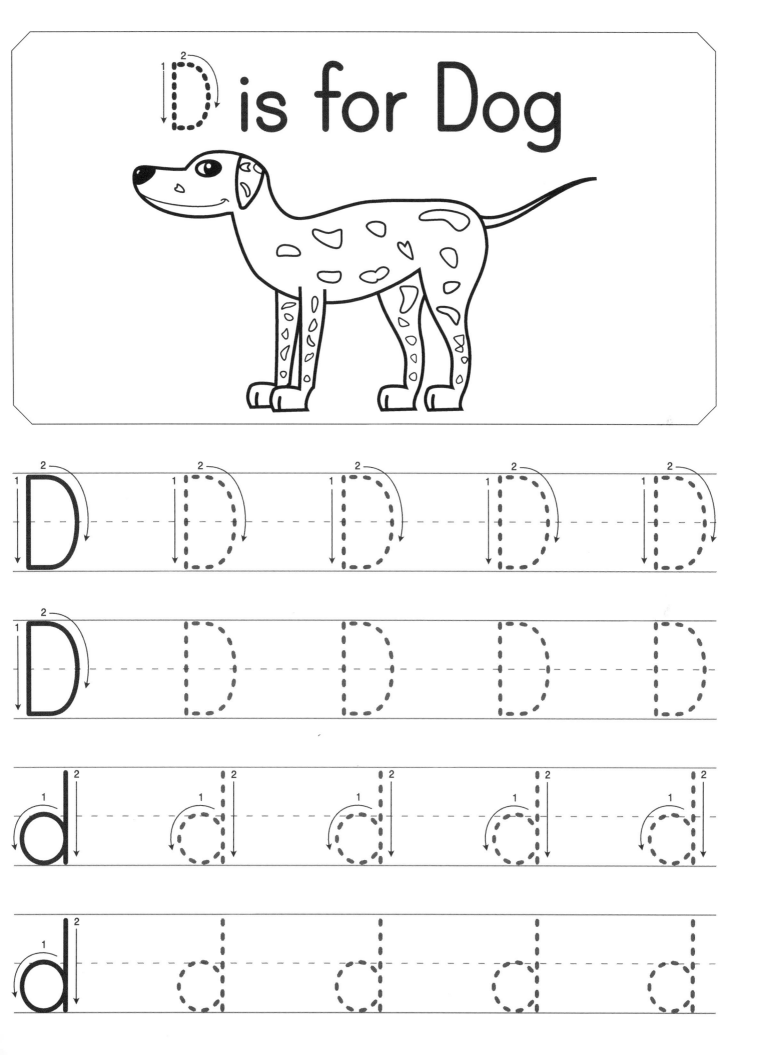

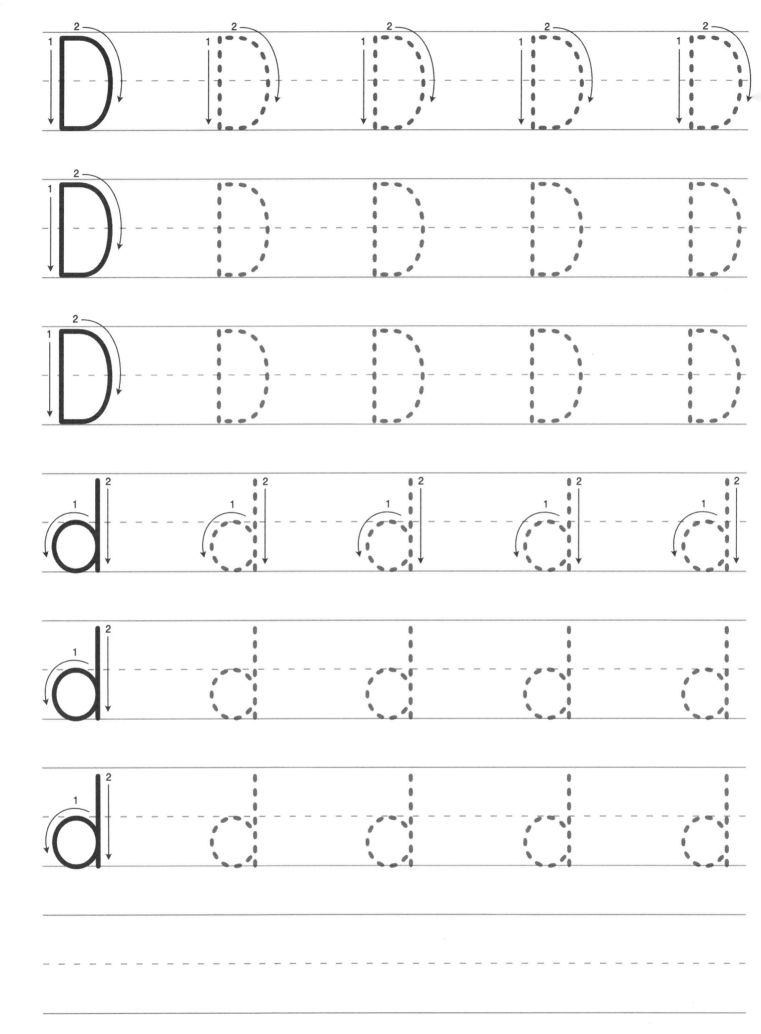

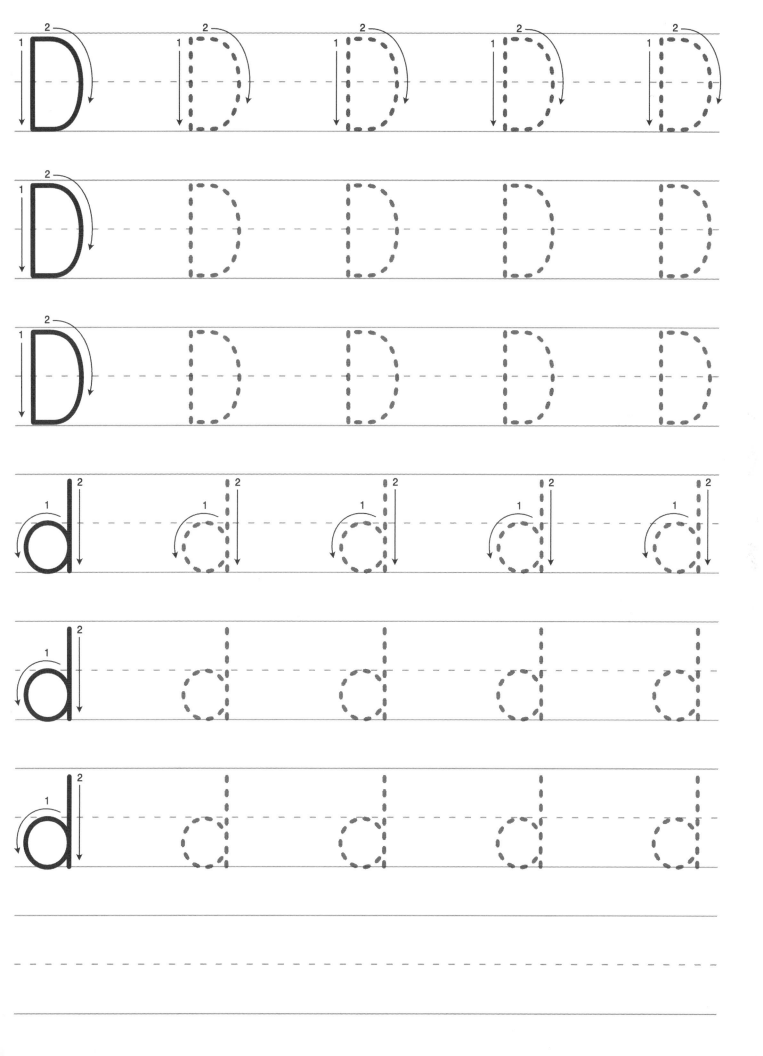

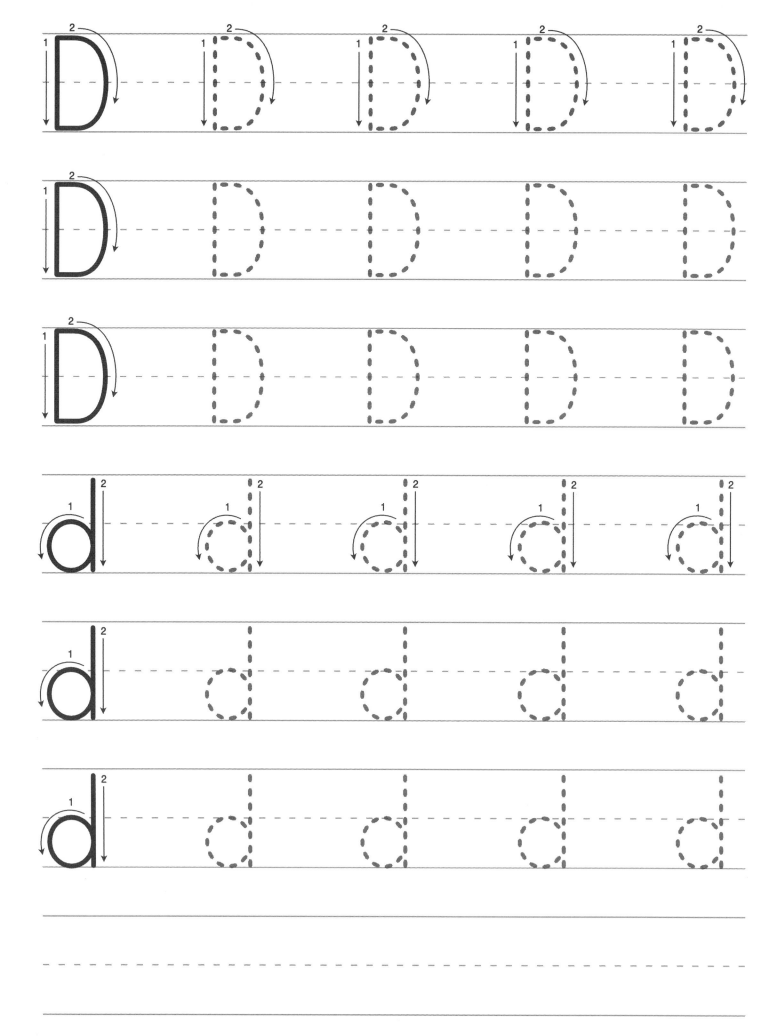

E is for Elephant

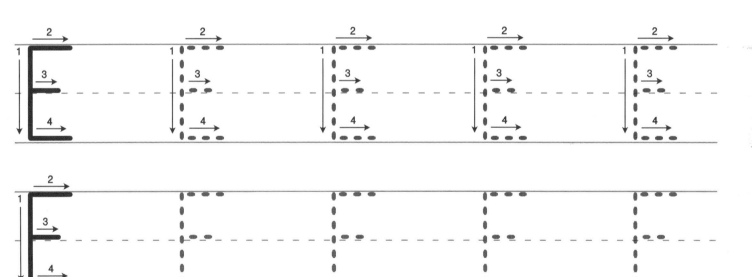

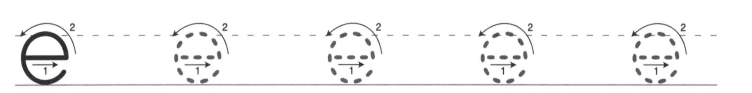

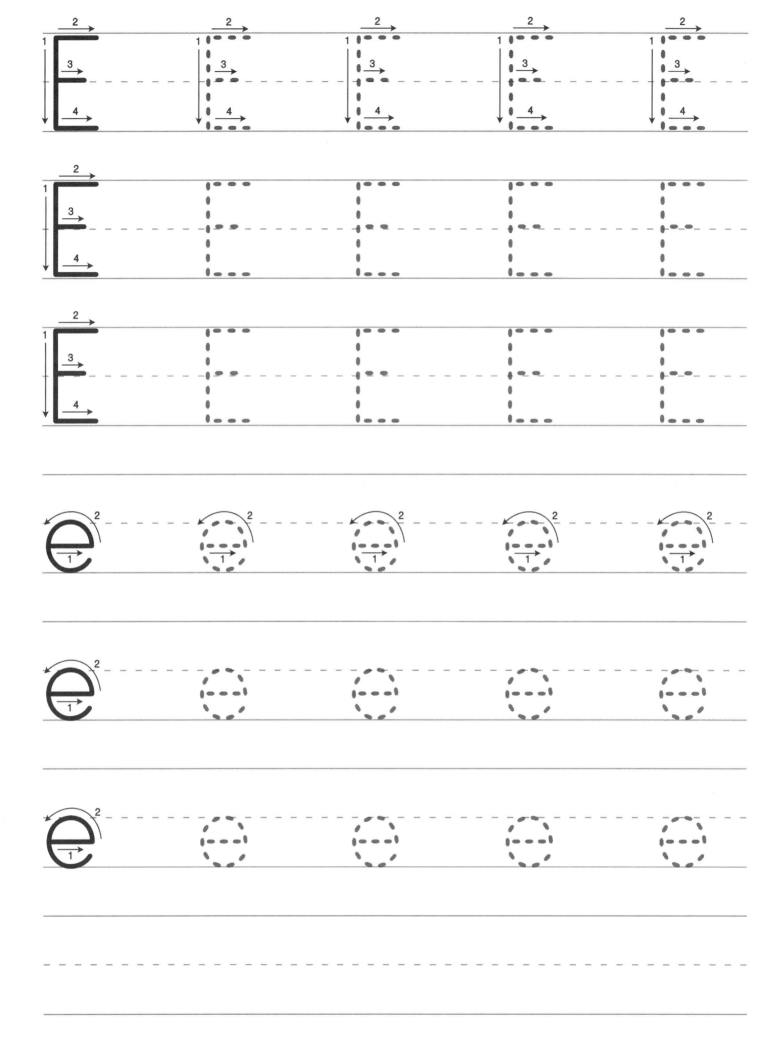

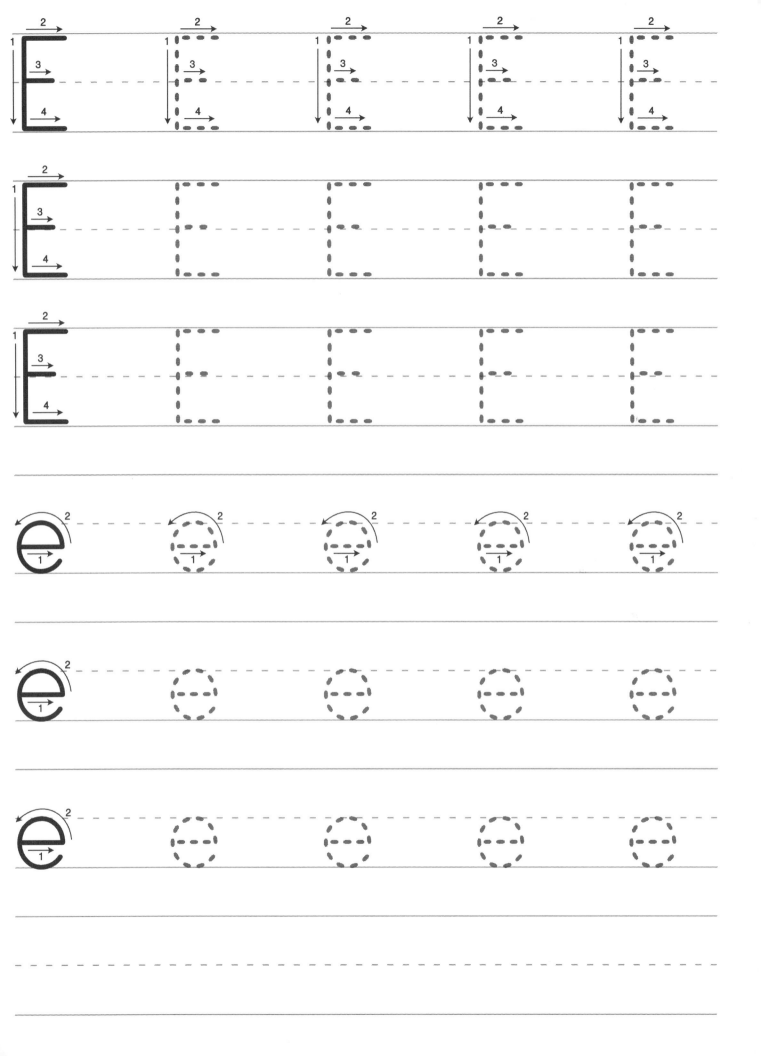

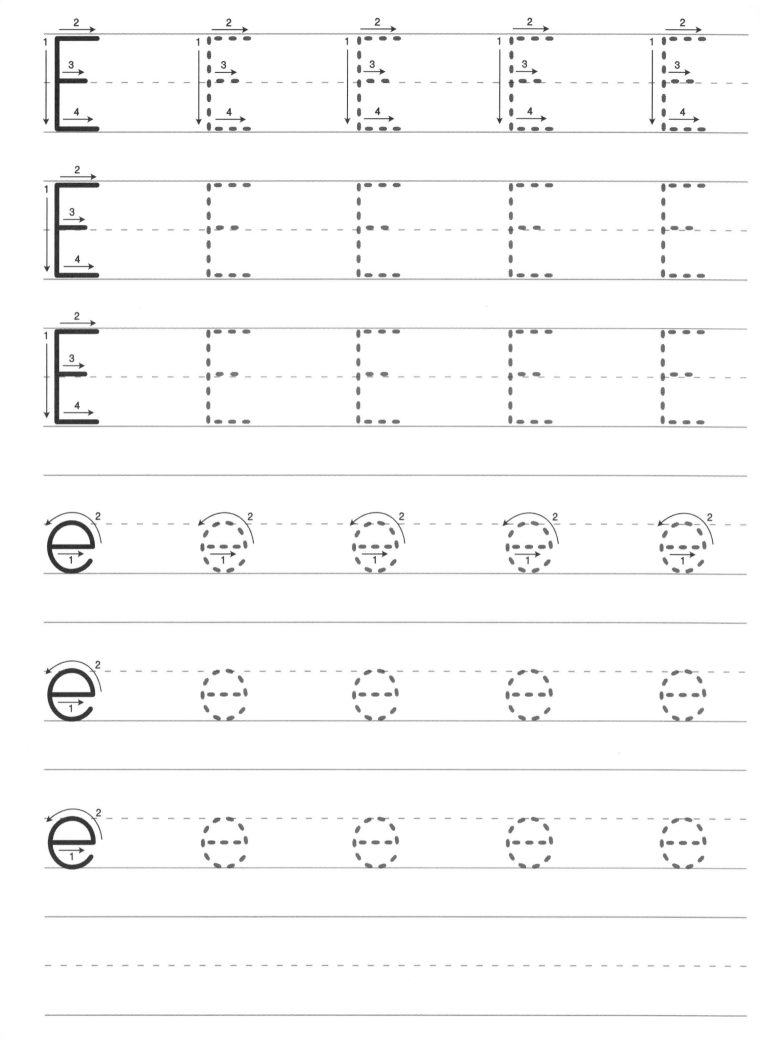

F is for Frog

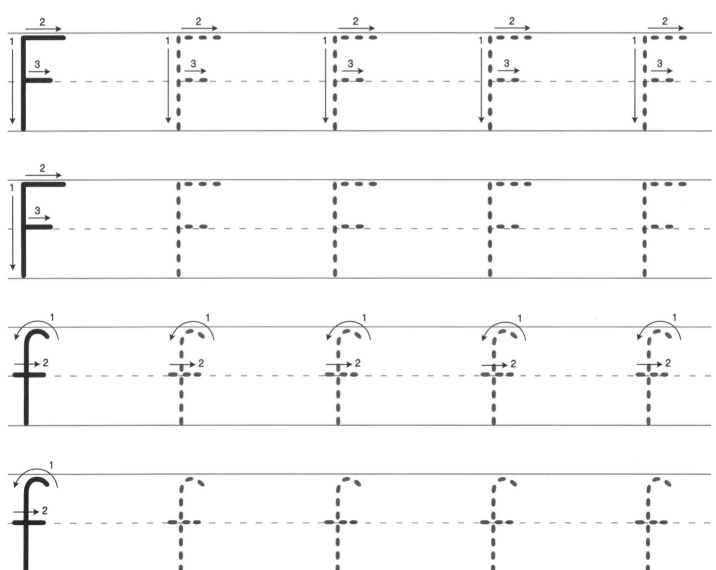

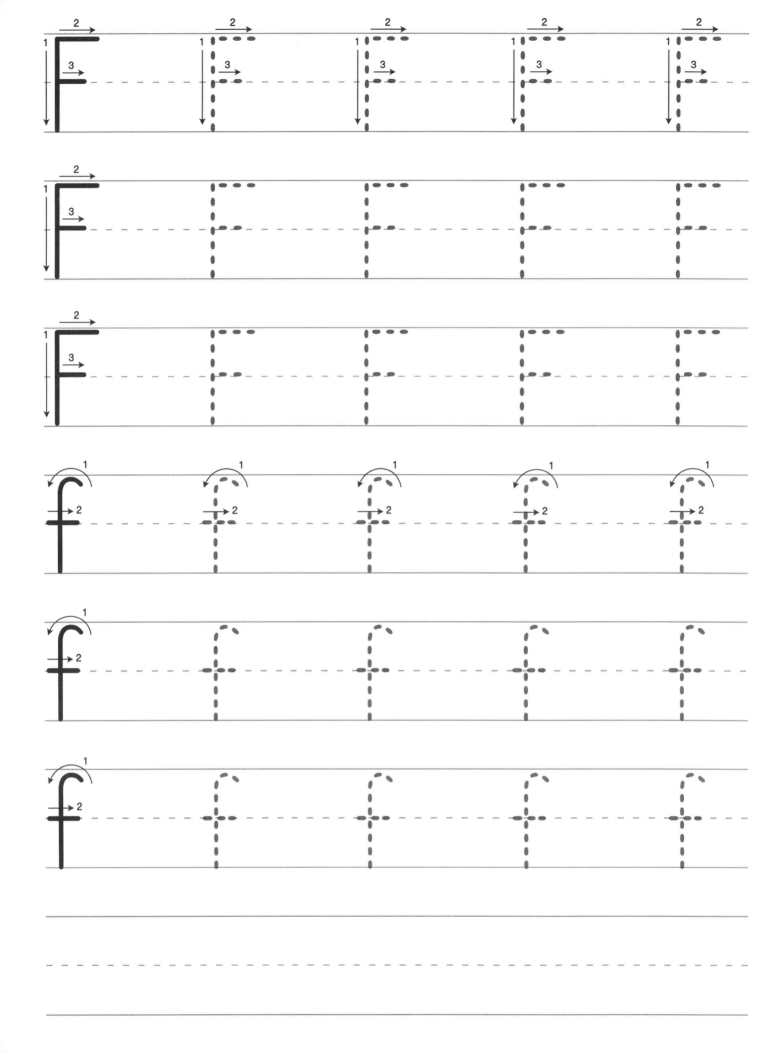

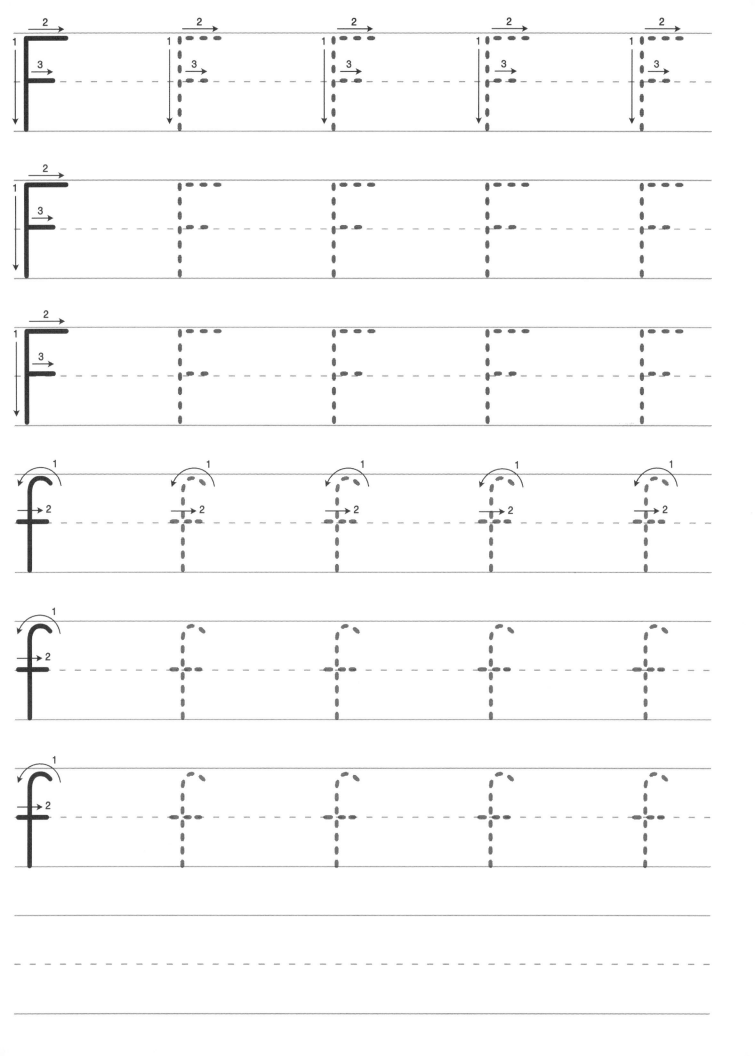

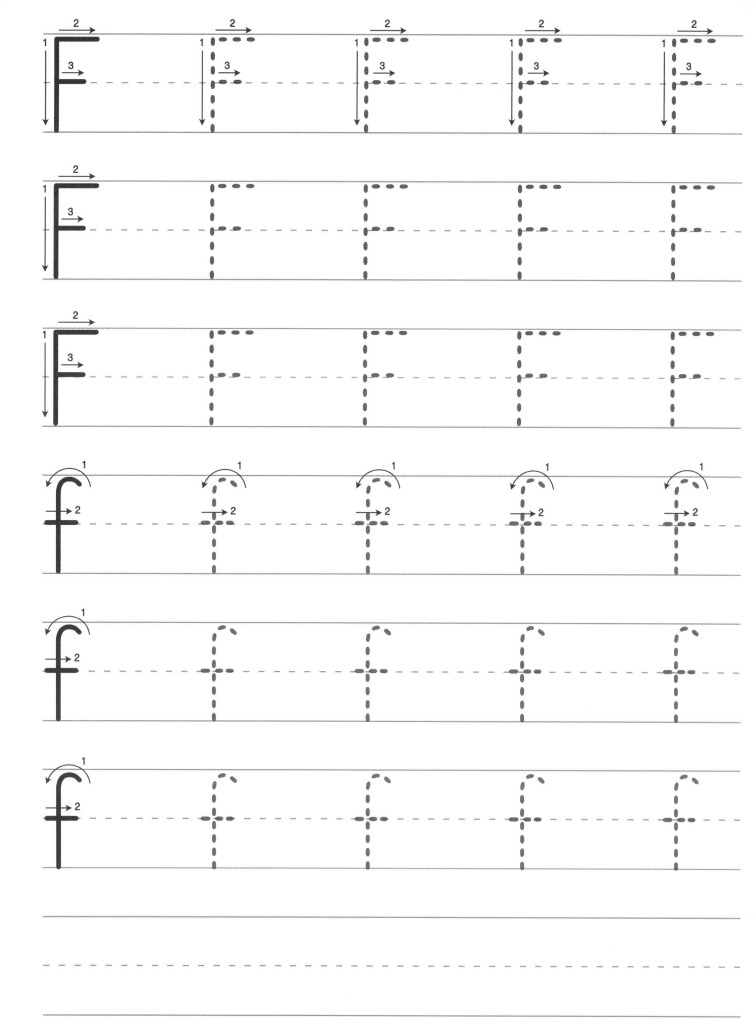

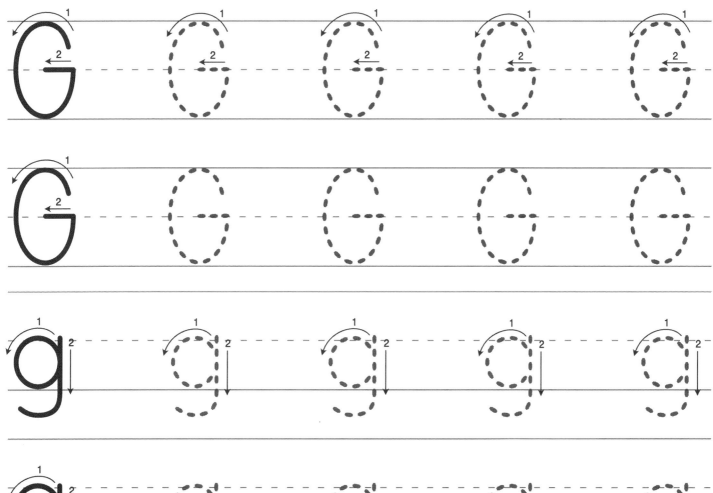

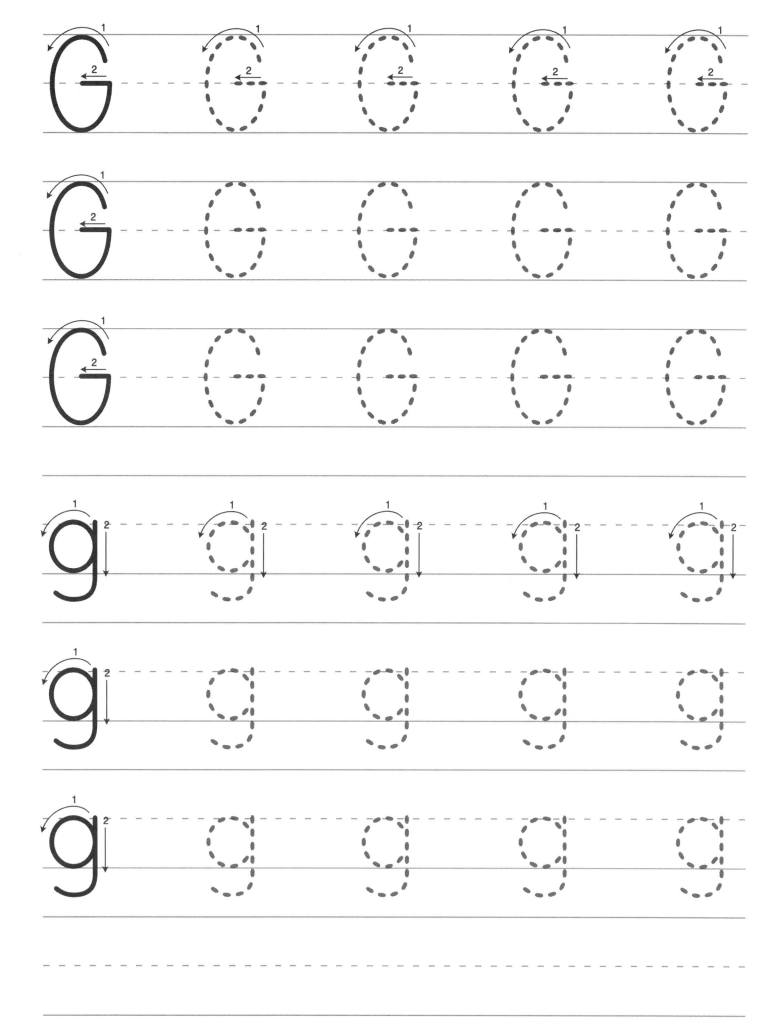

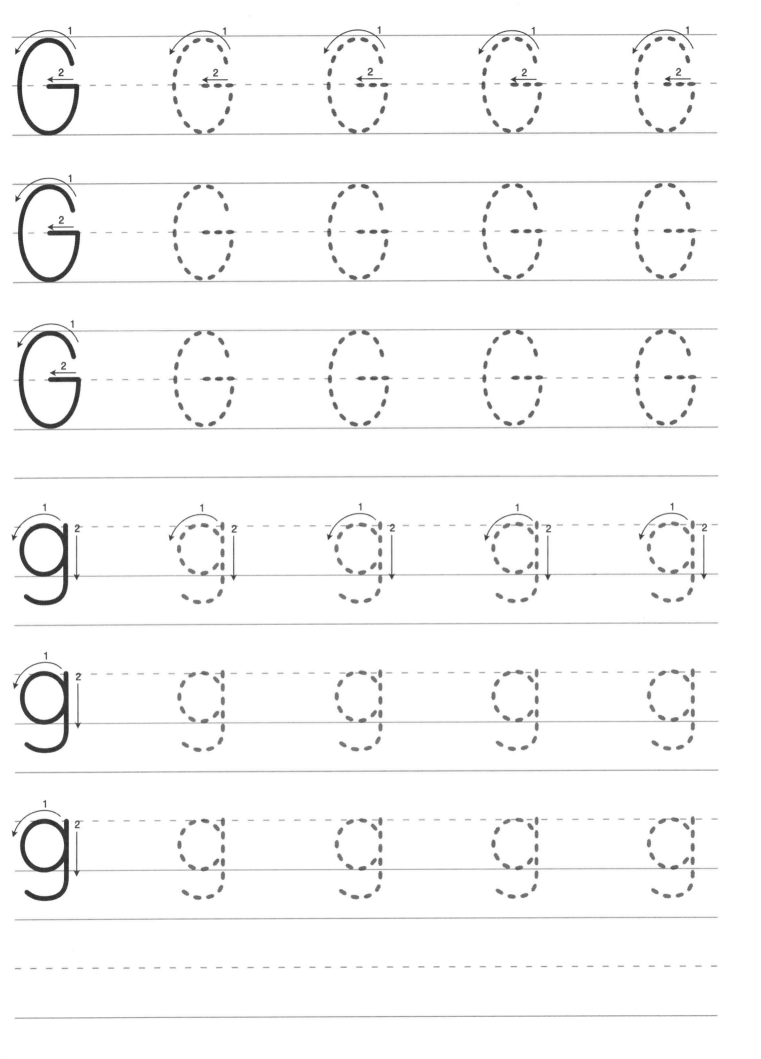

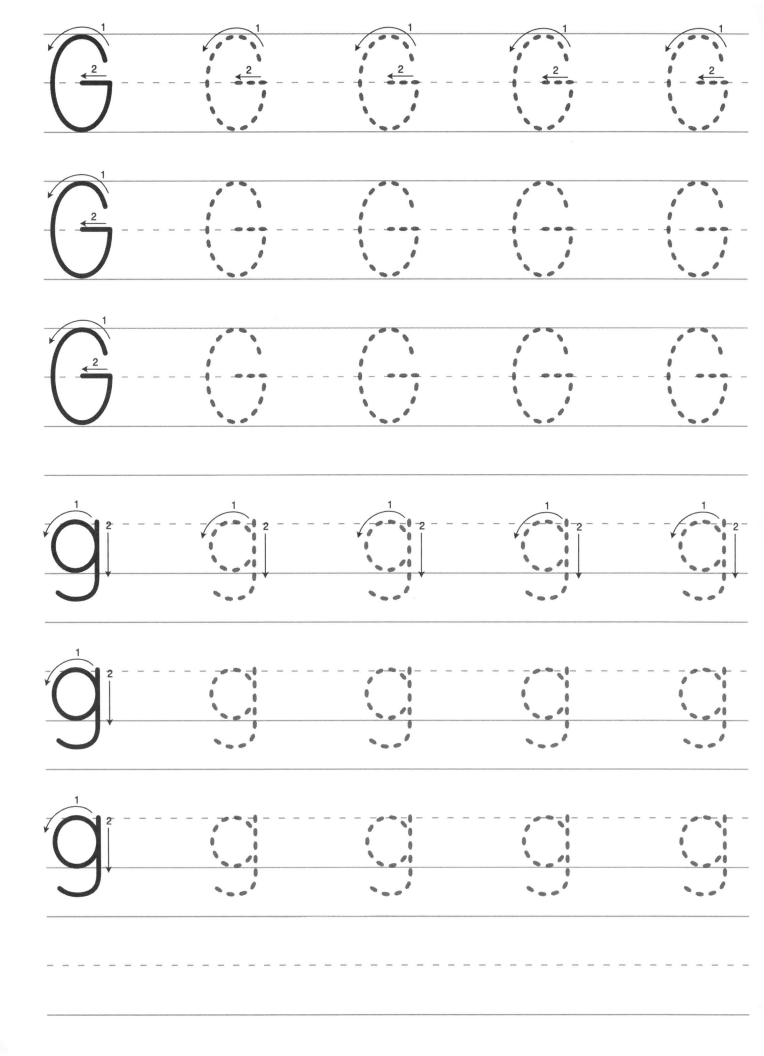

H is for Home

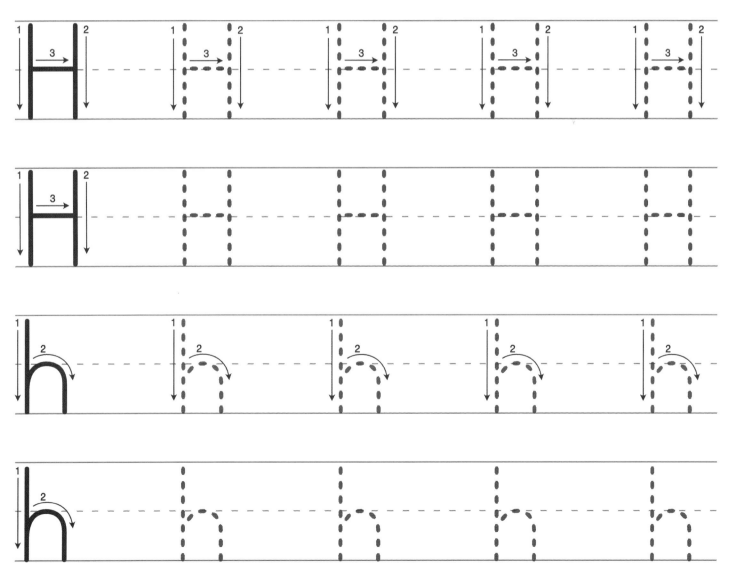

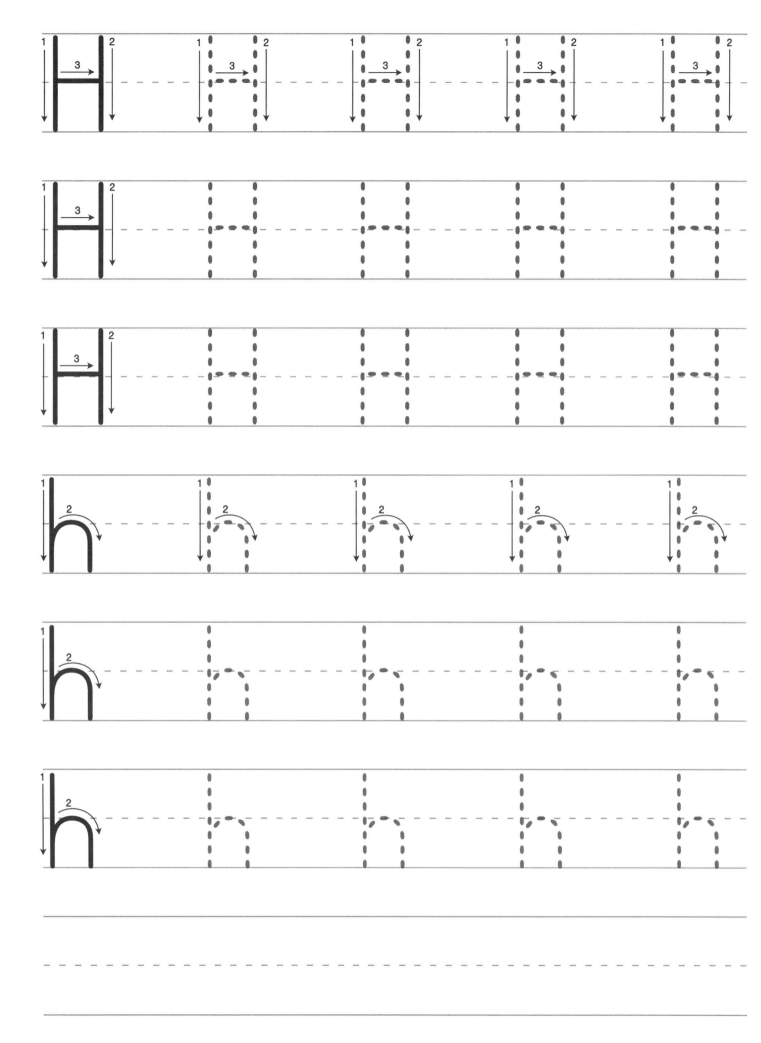

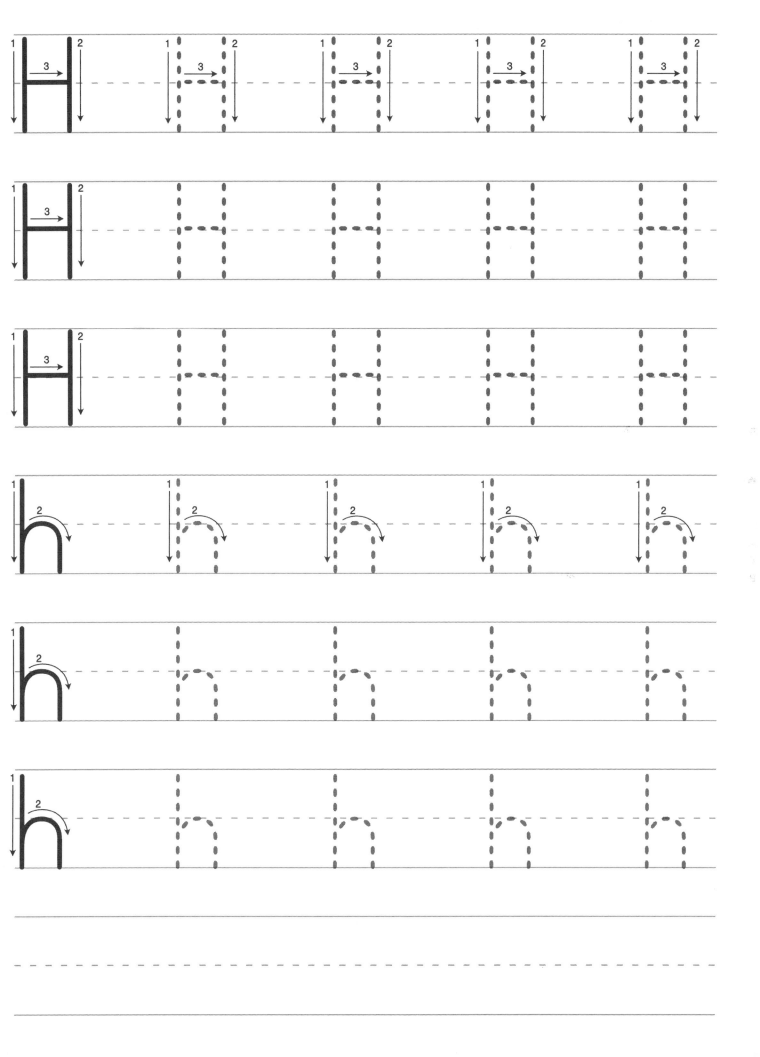

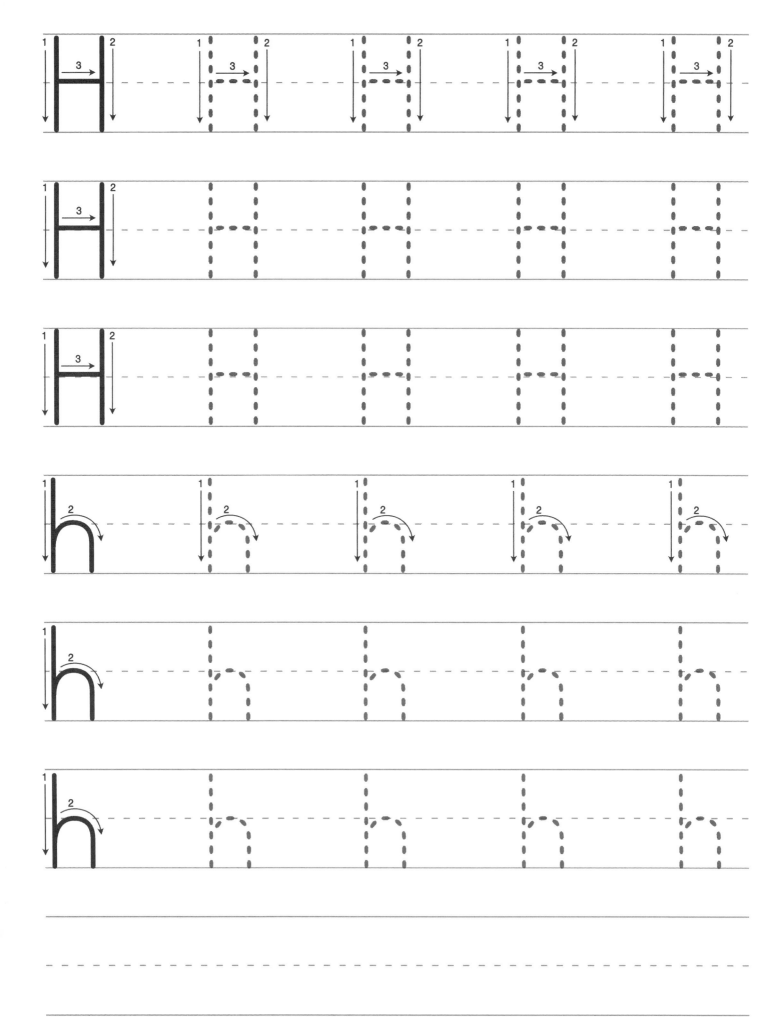

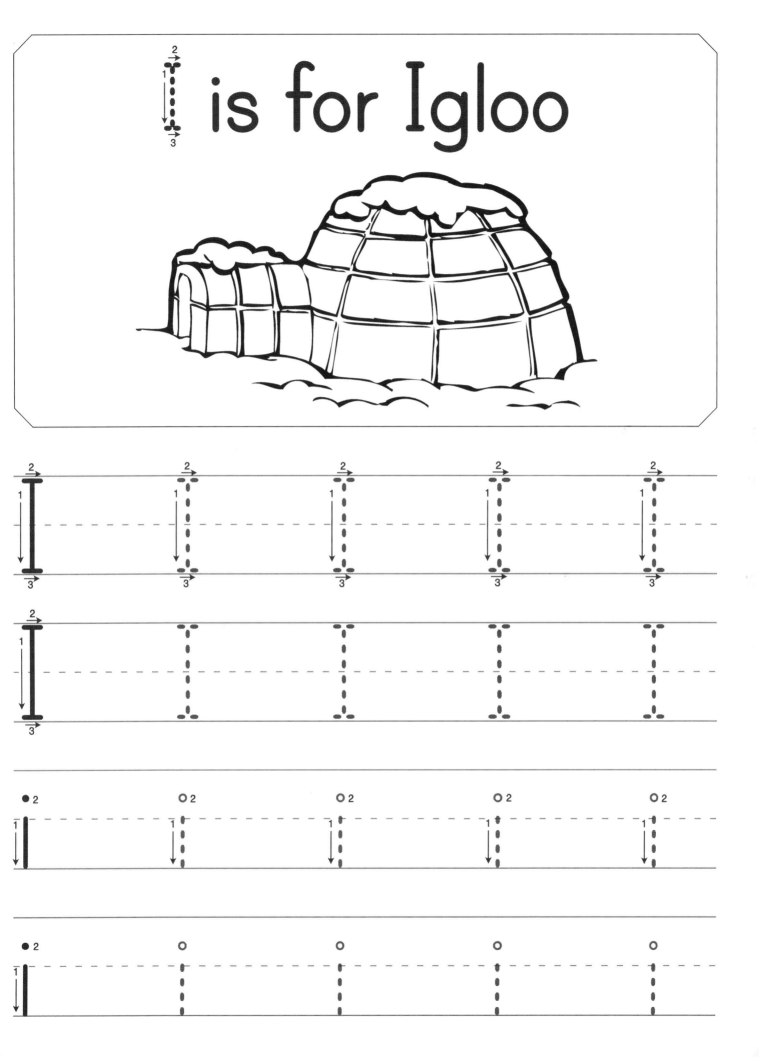

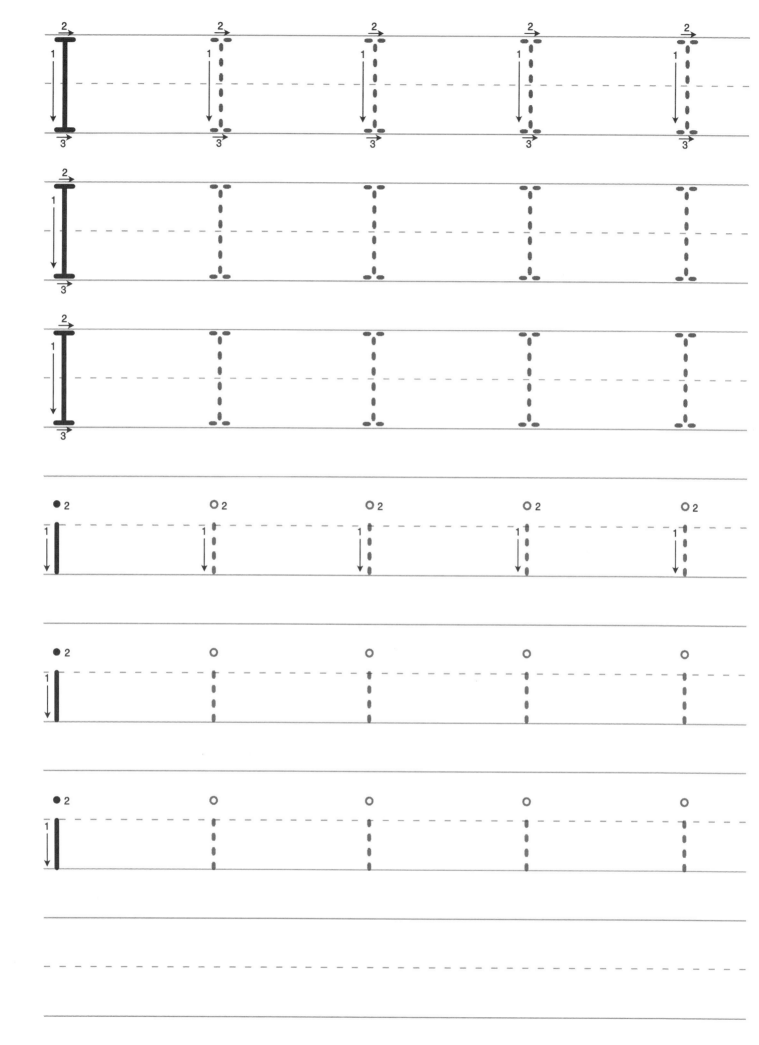

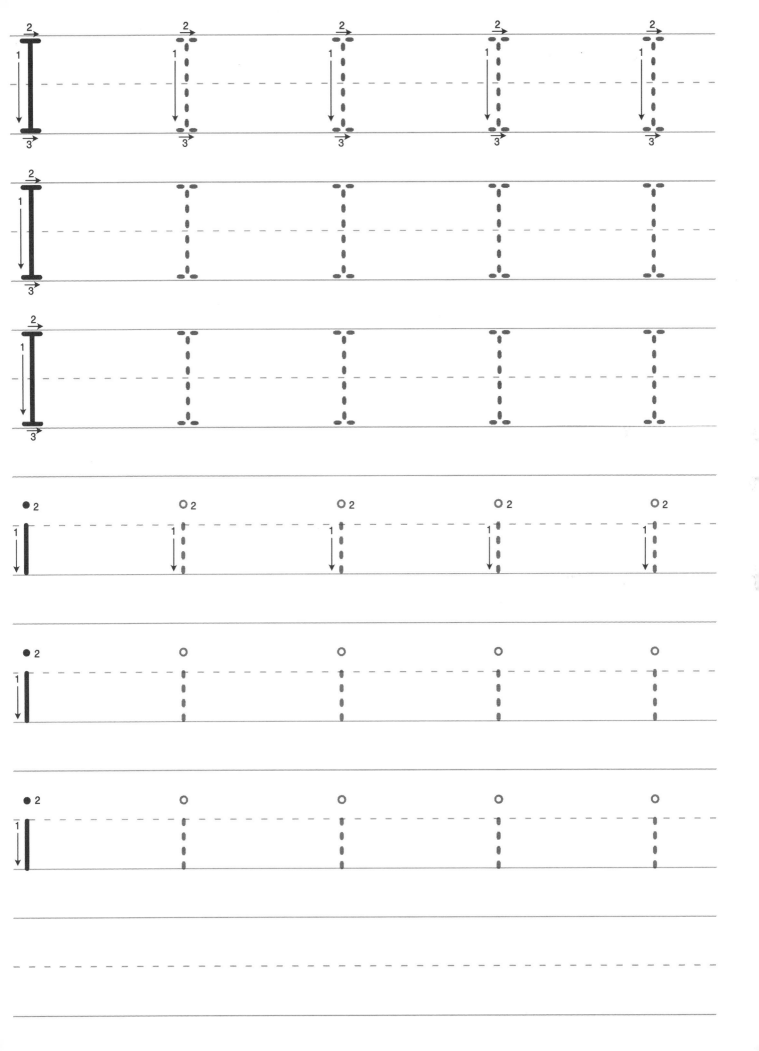

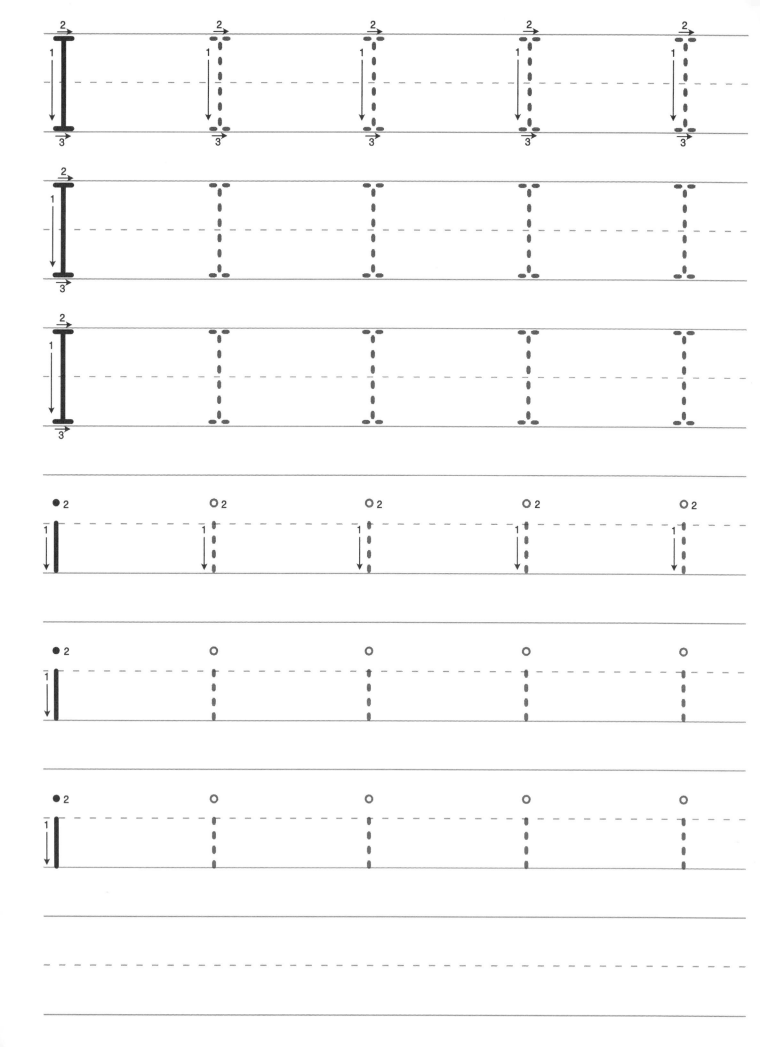

J is for Jellyfish

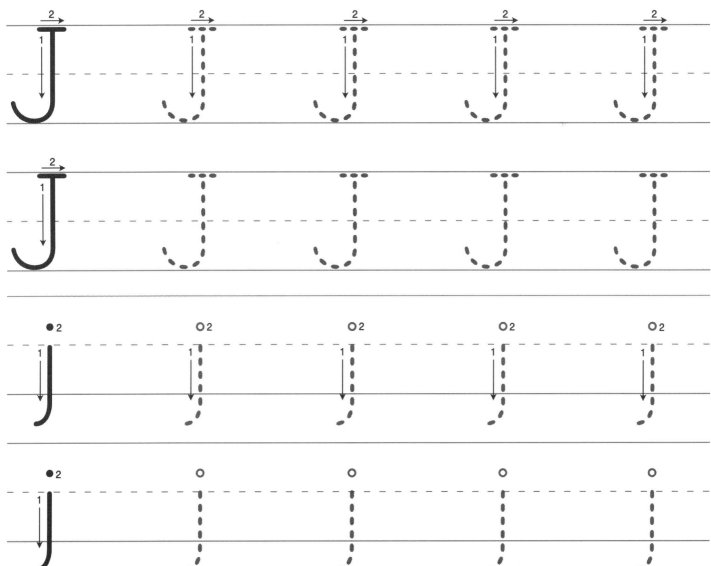

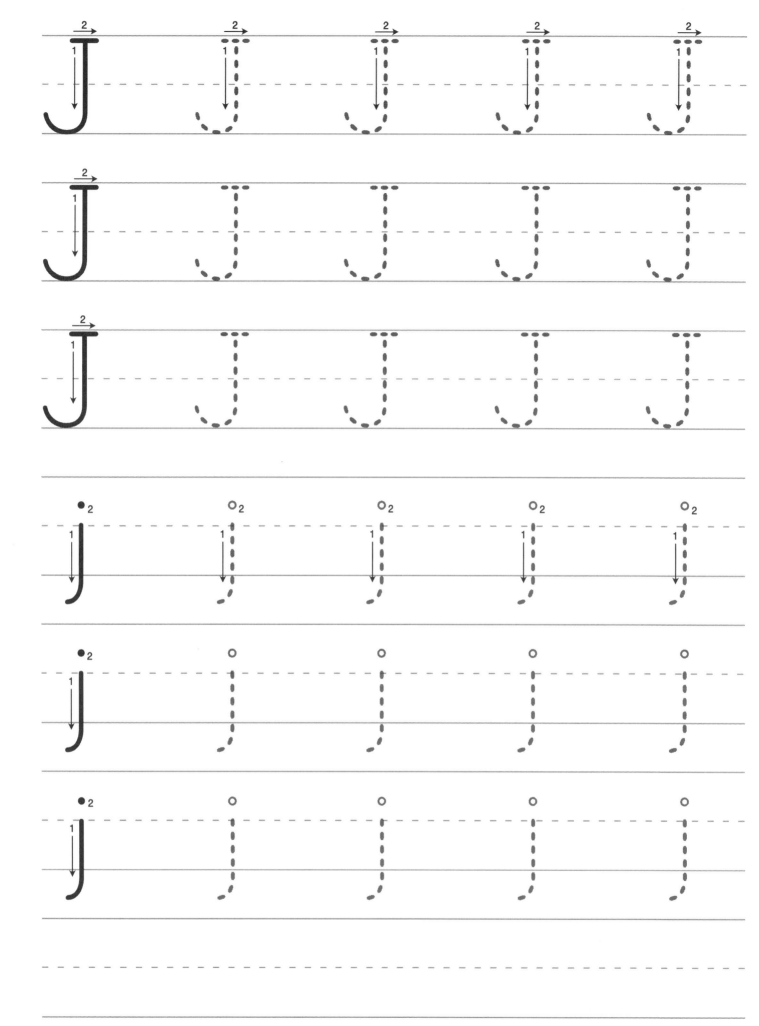

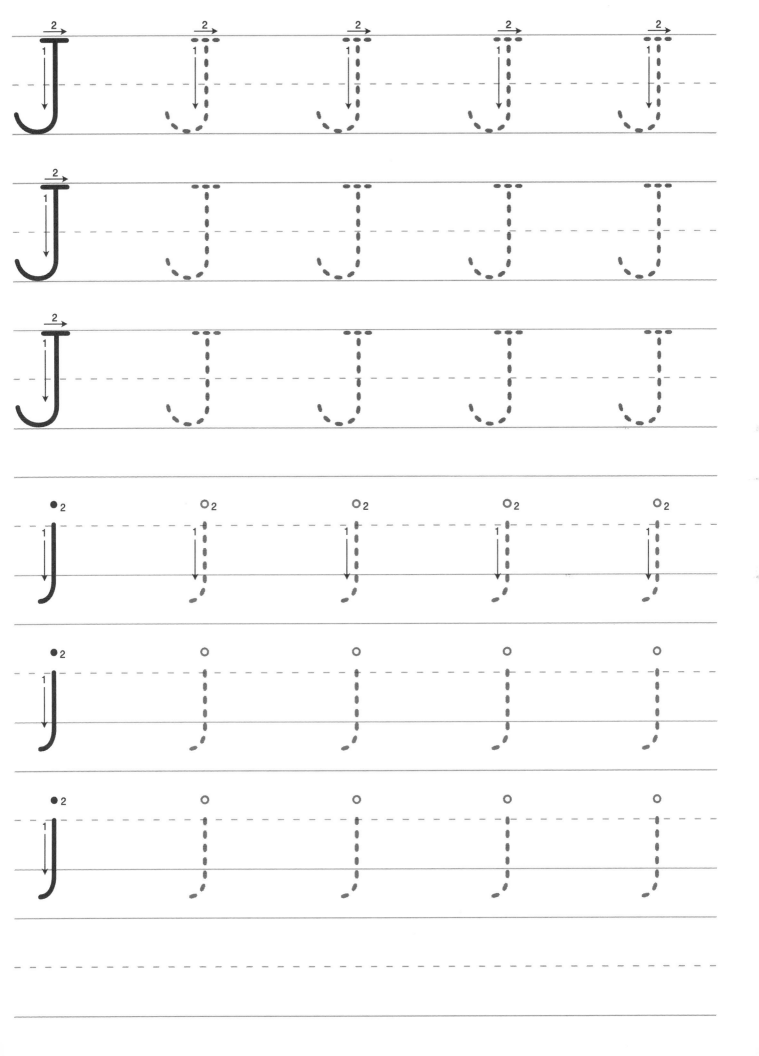

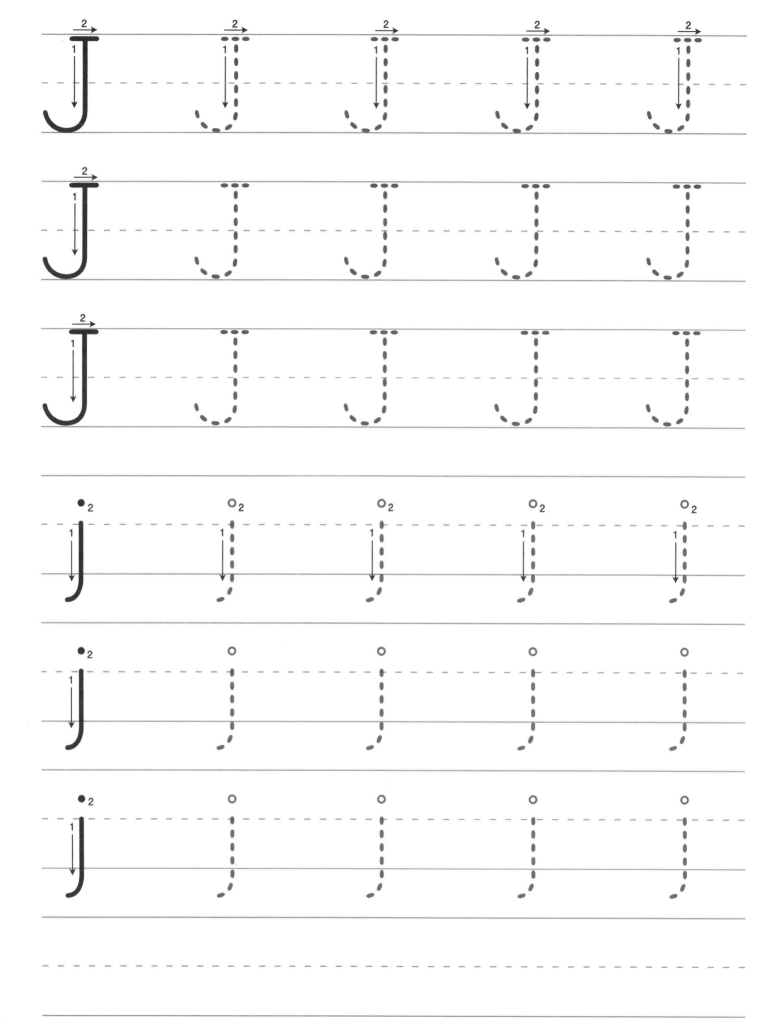

K is for Kangaroo

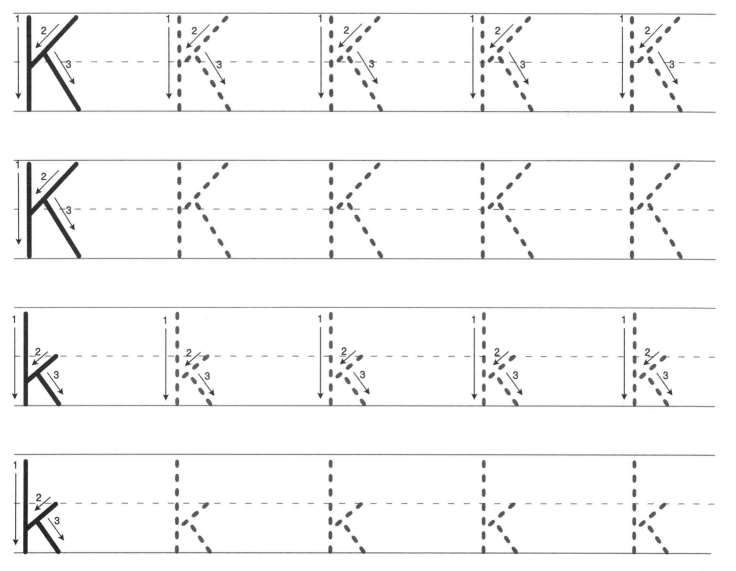

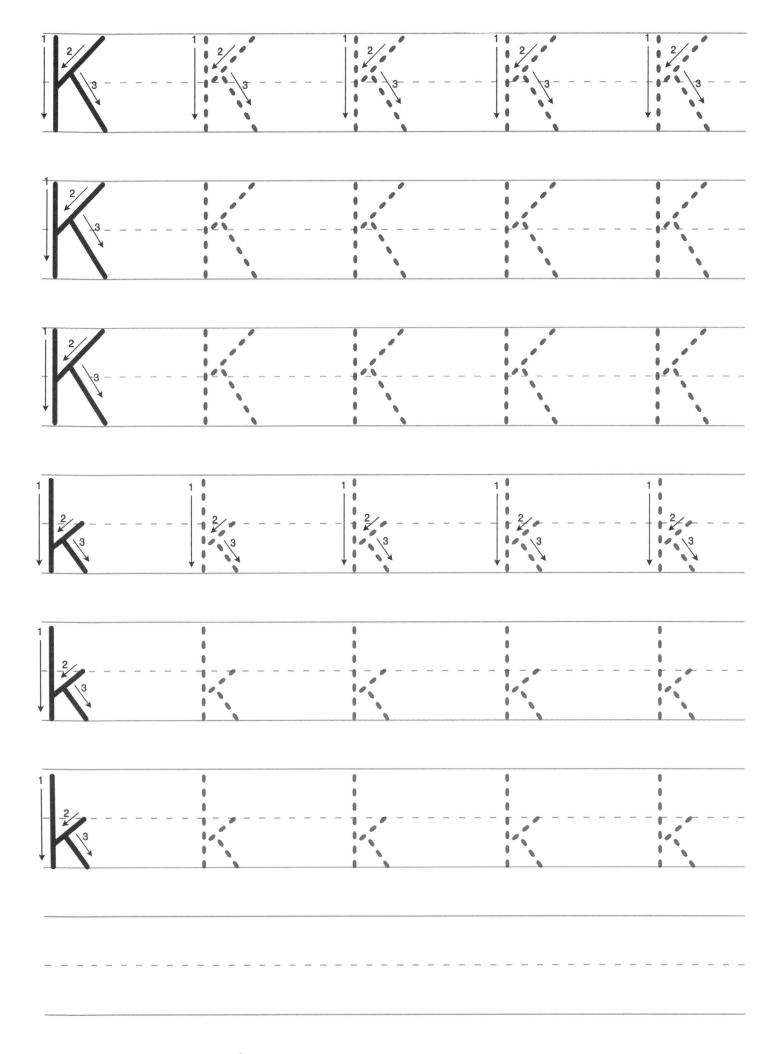

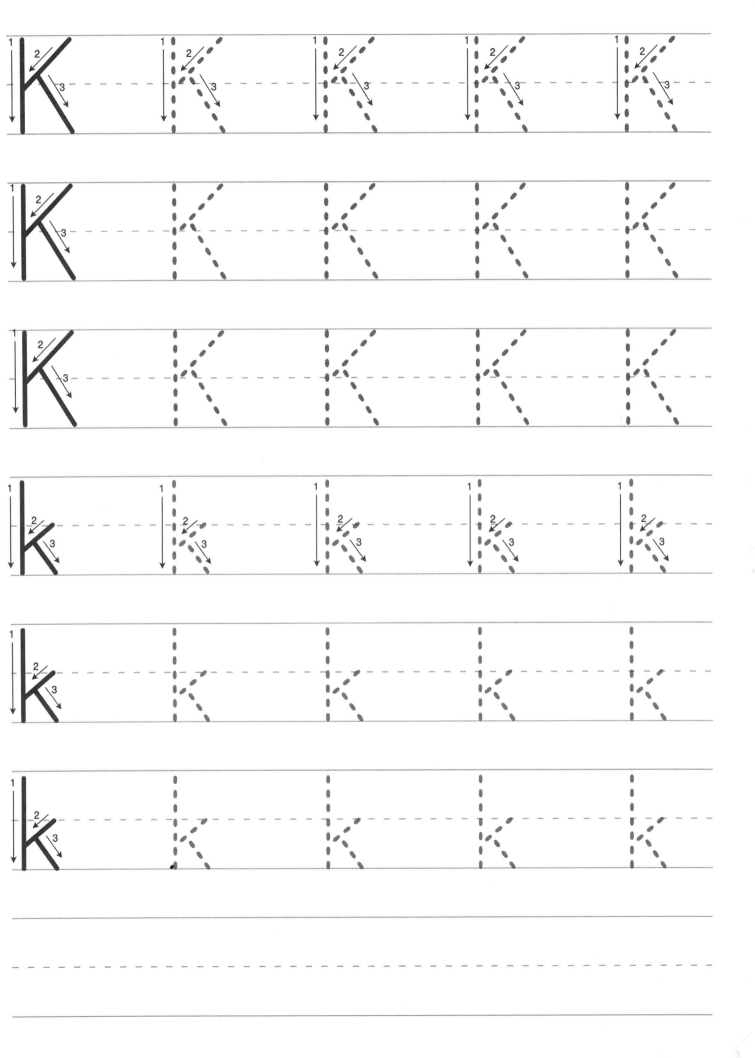

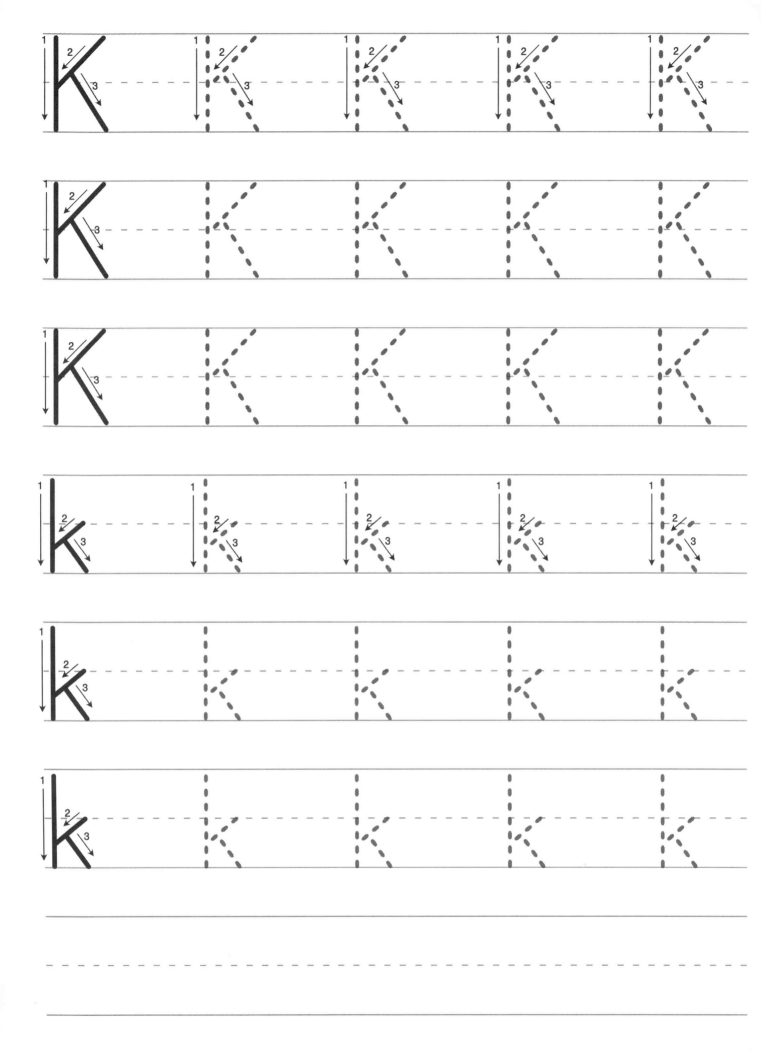

L is for Lion

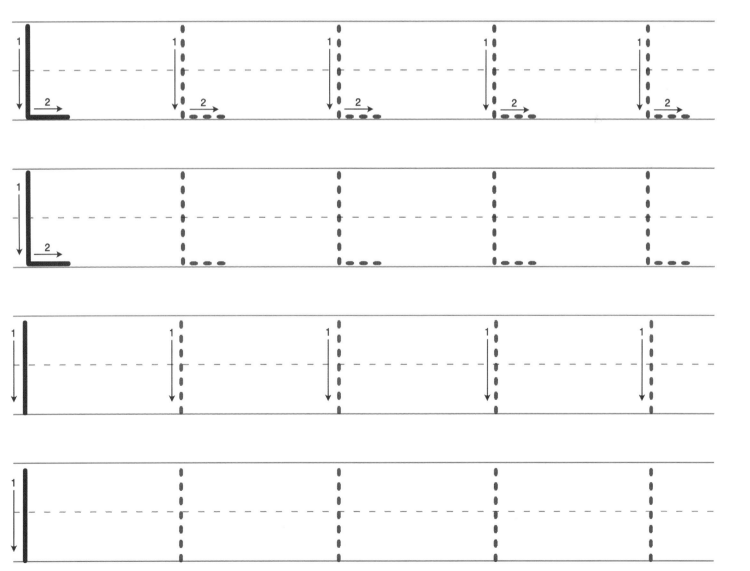

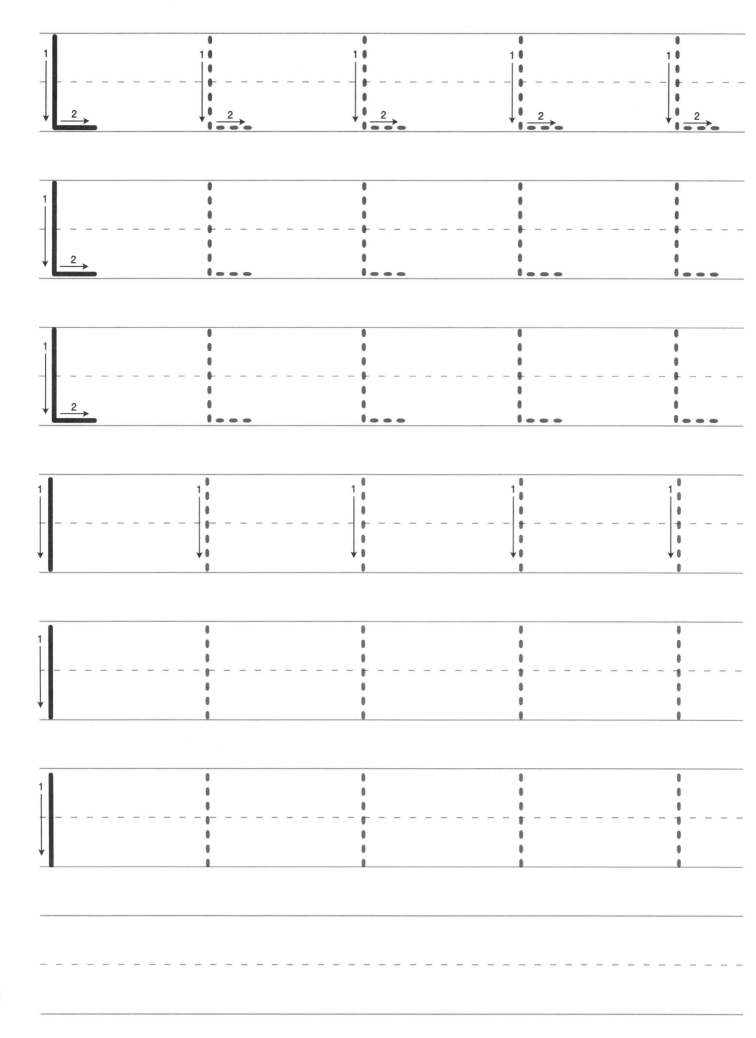

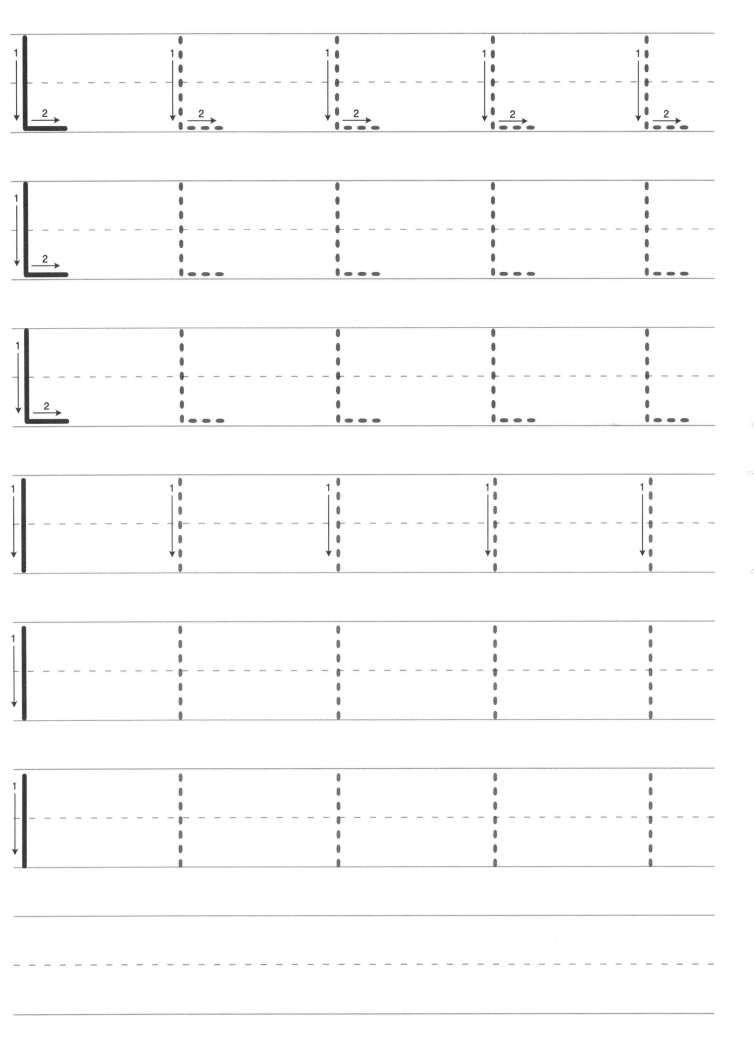

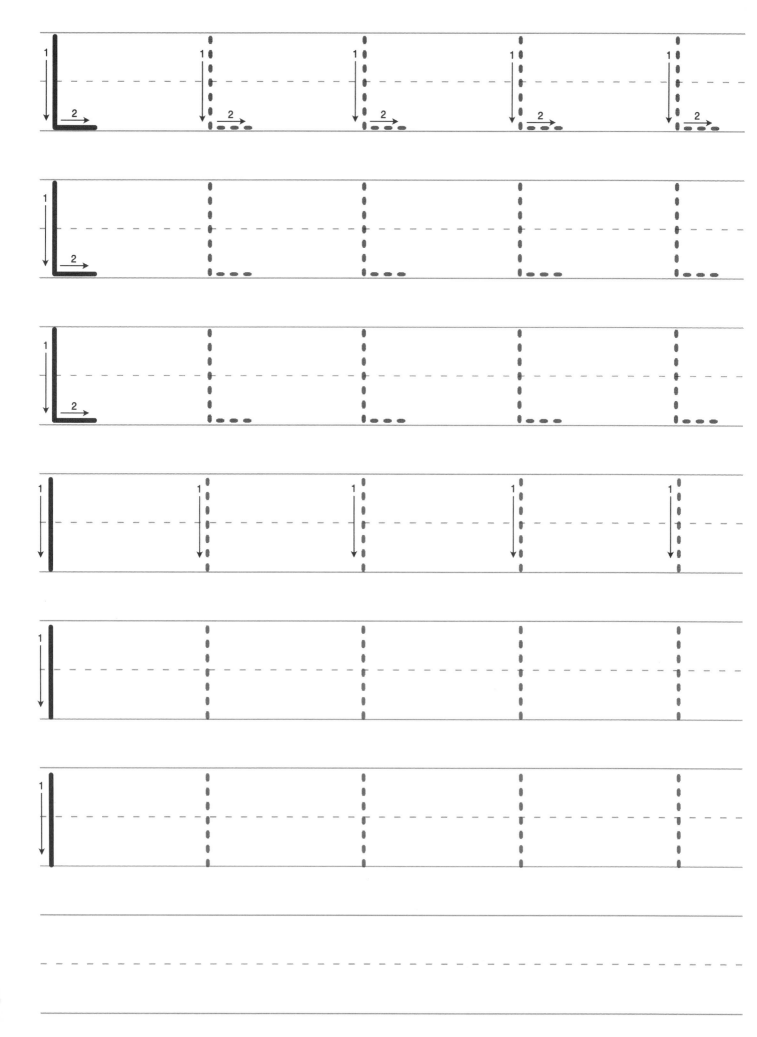

 M is for Mushroom

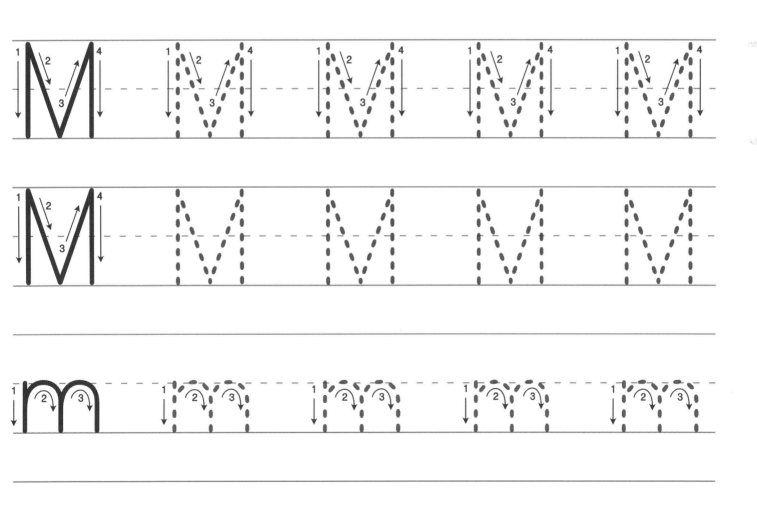

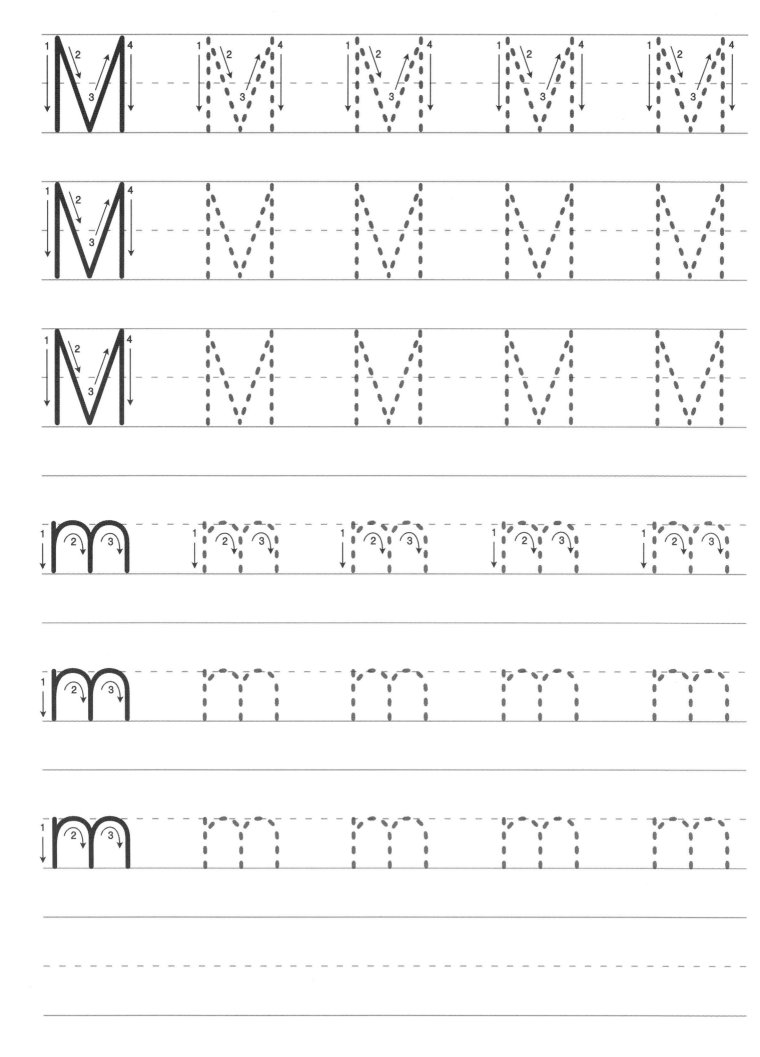

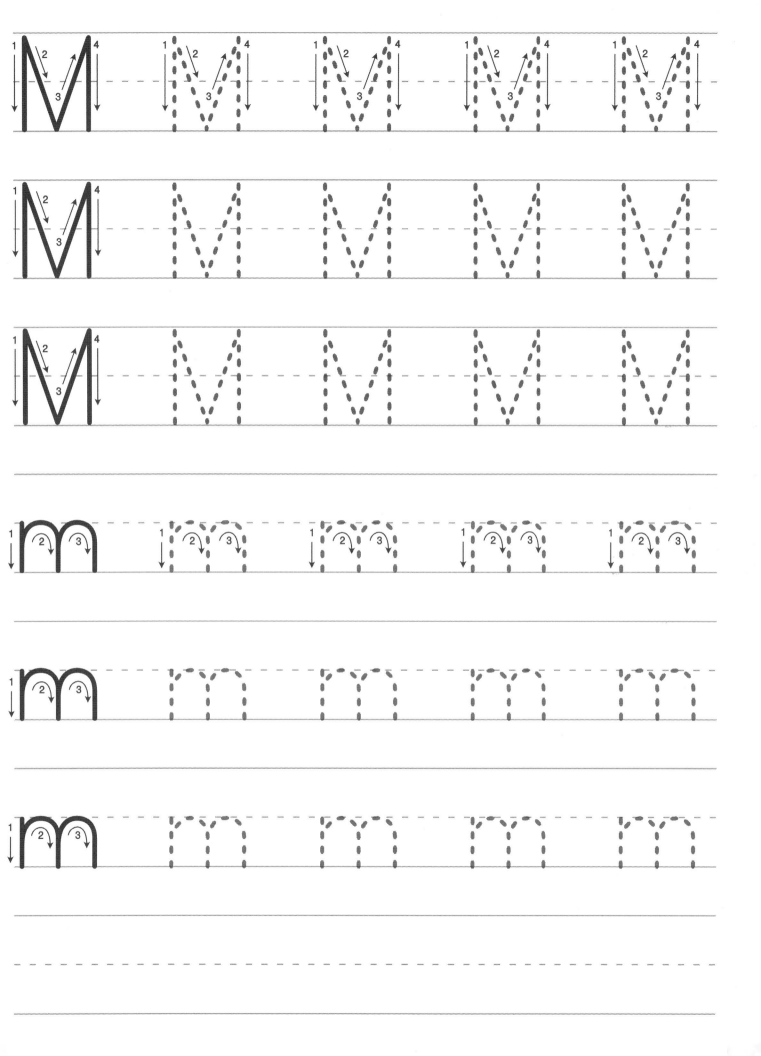

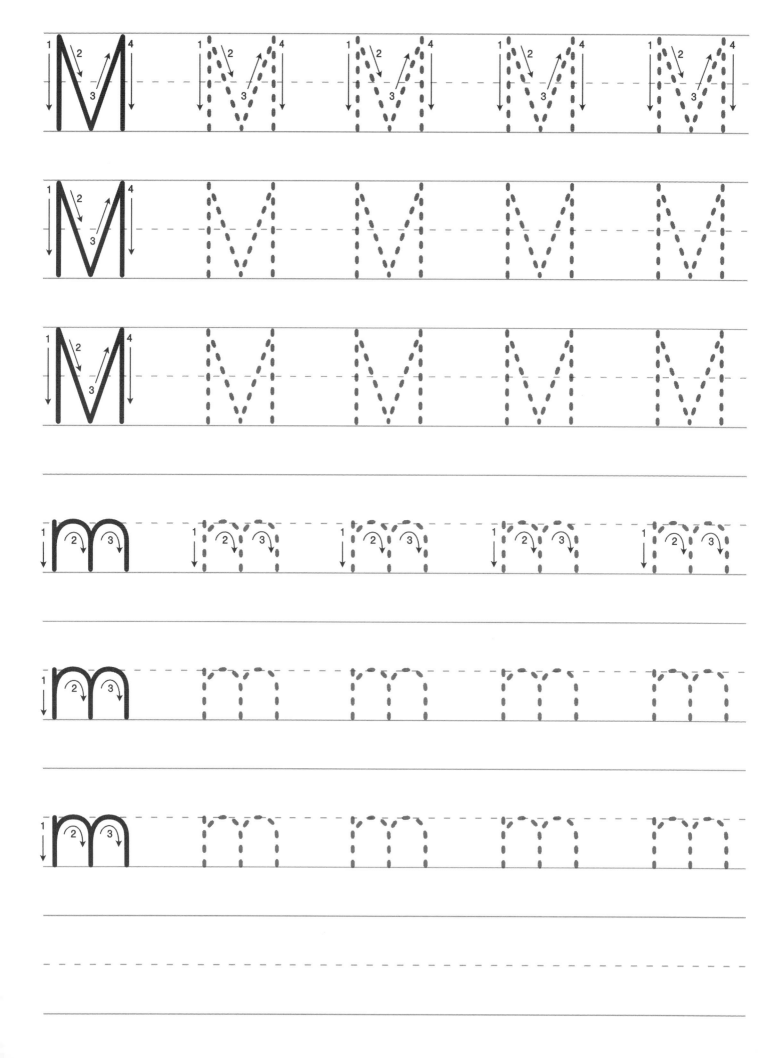

N is for Nest

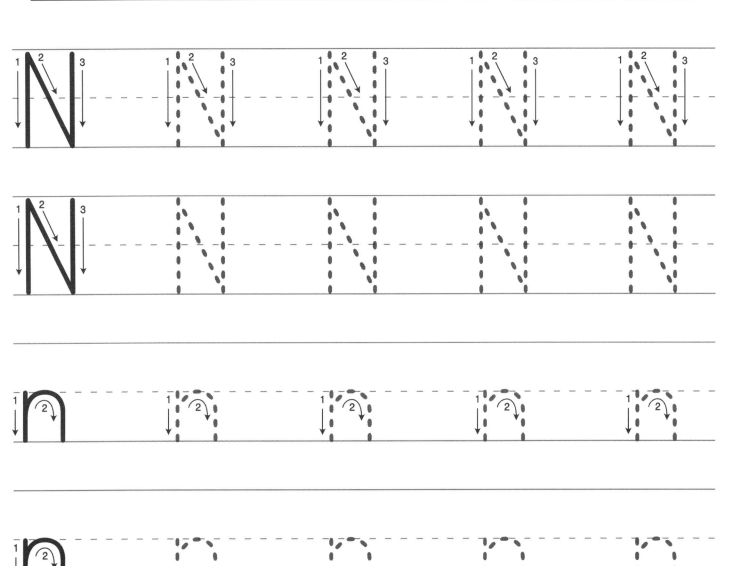

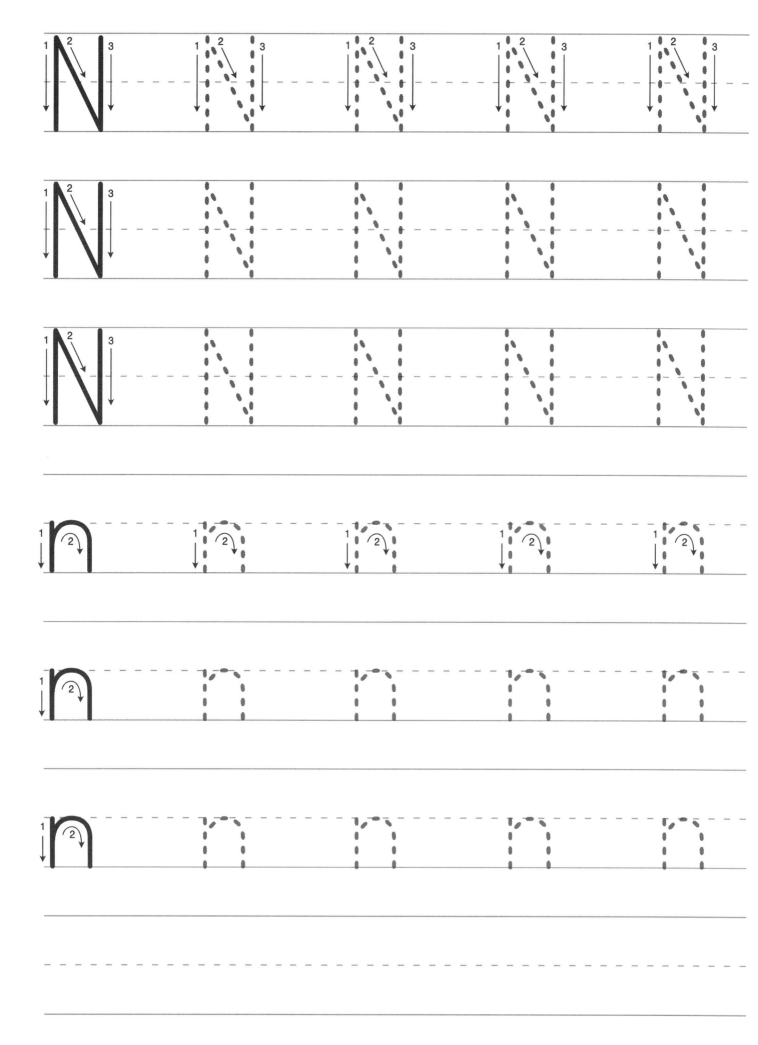

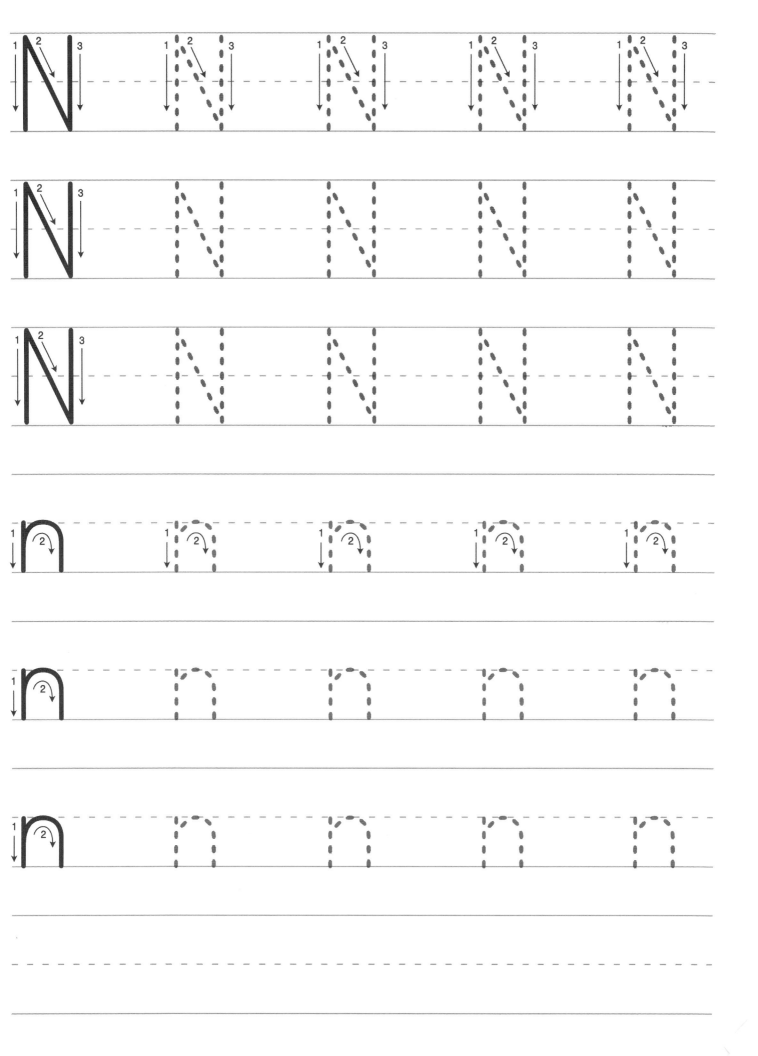

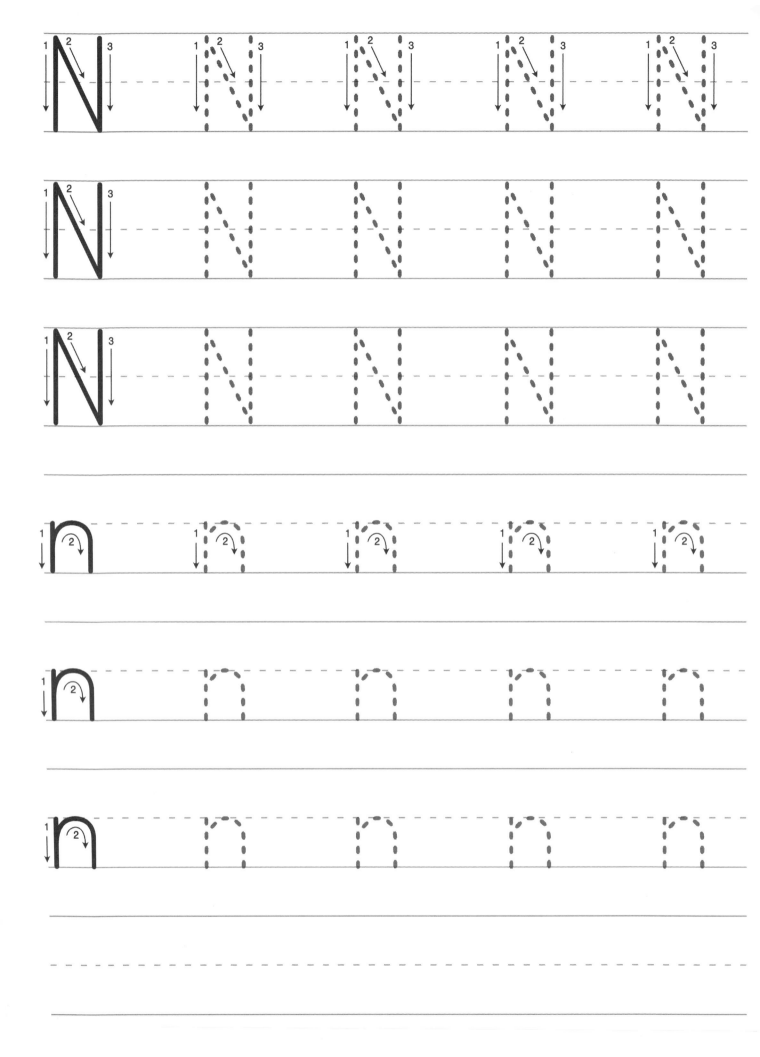

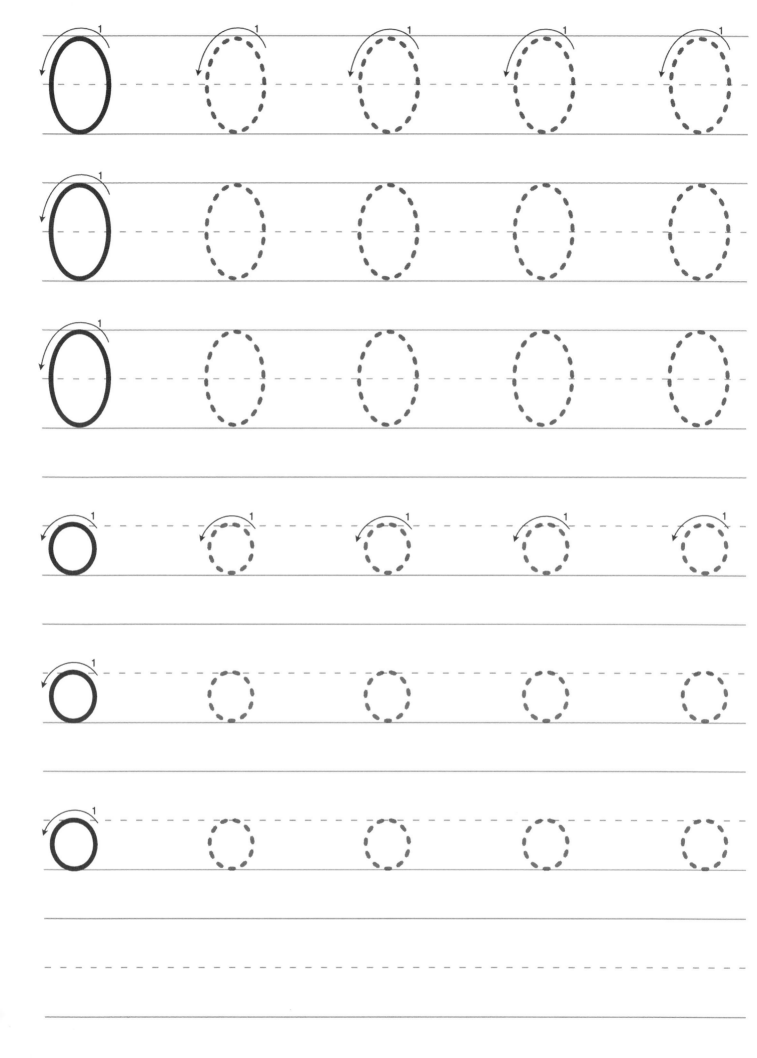

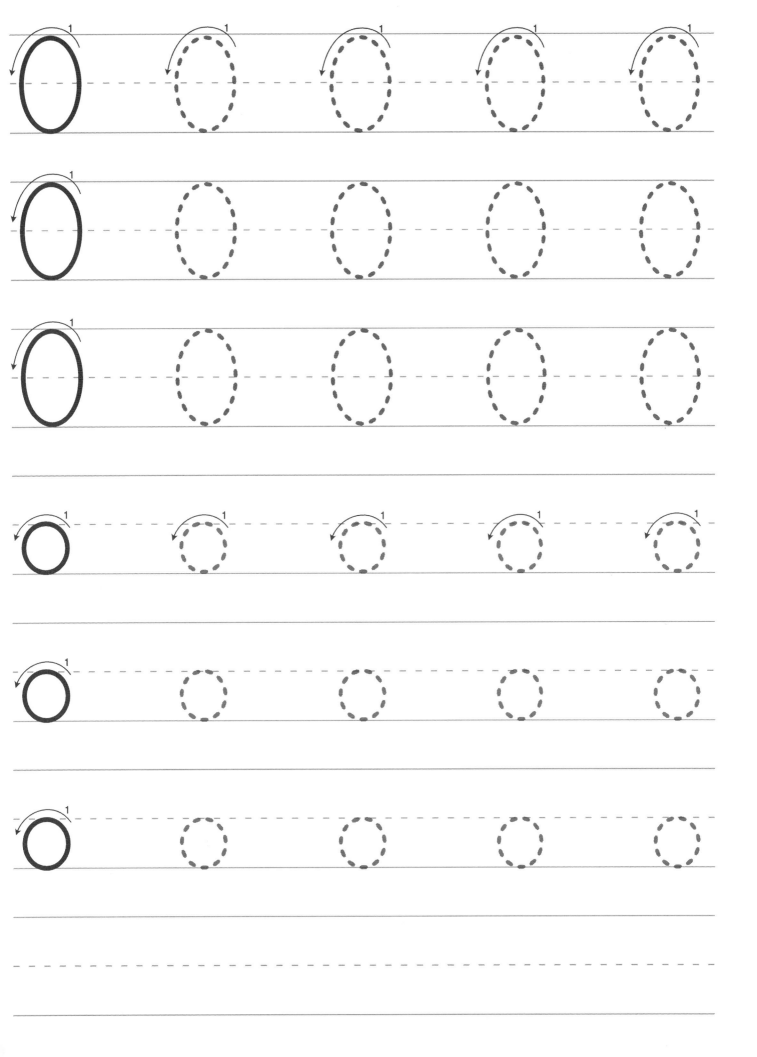

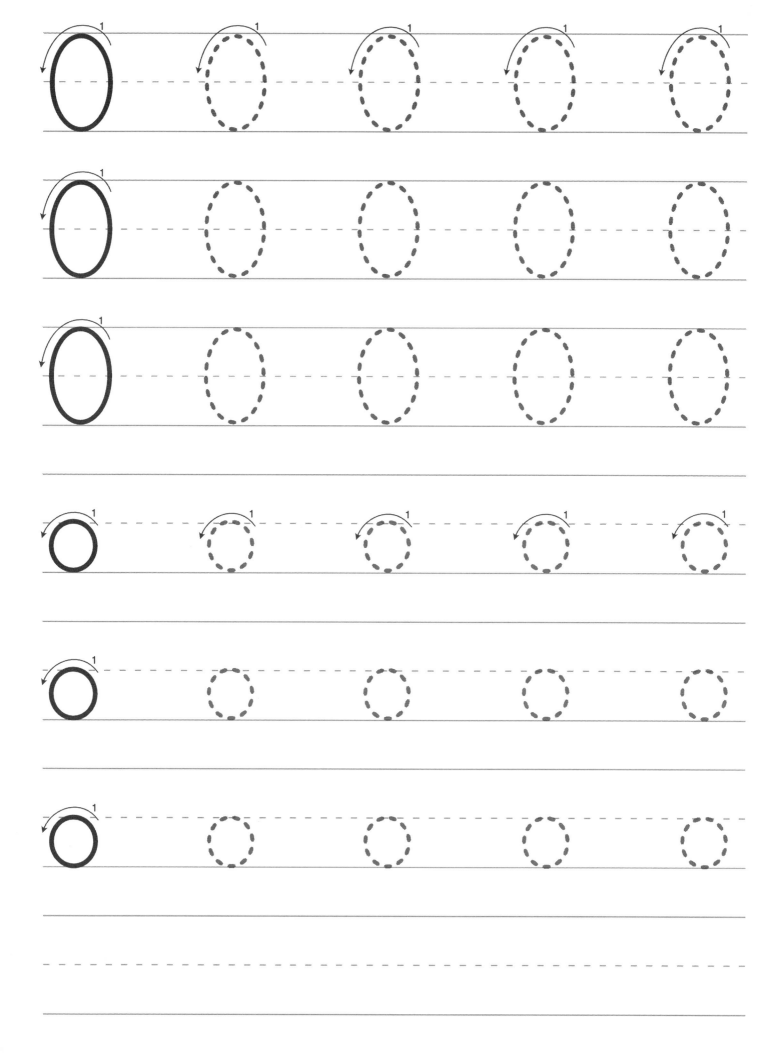

P is for Pig

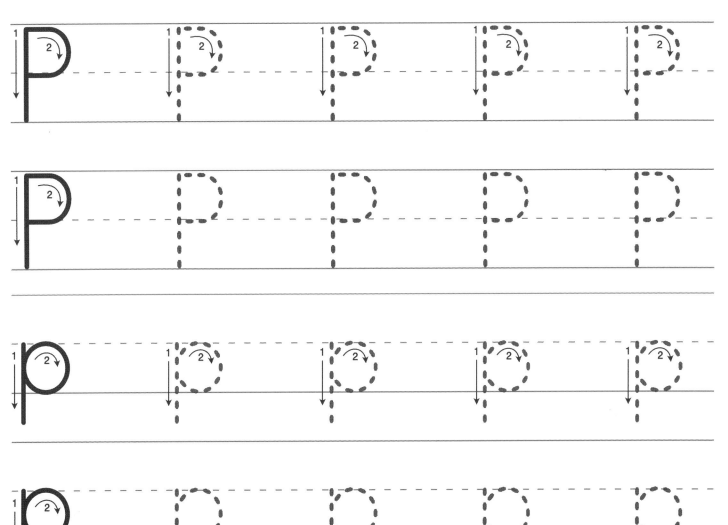

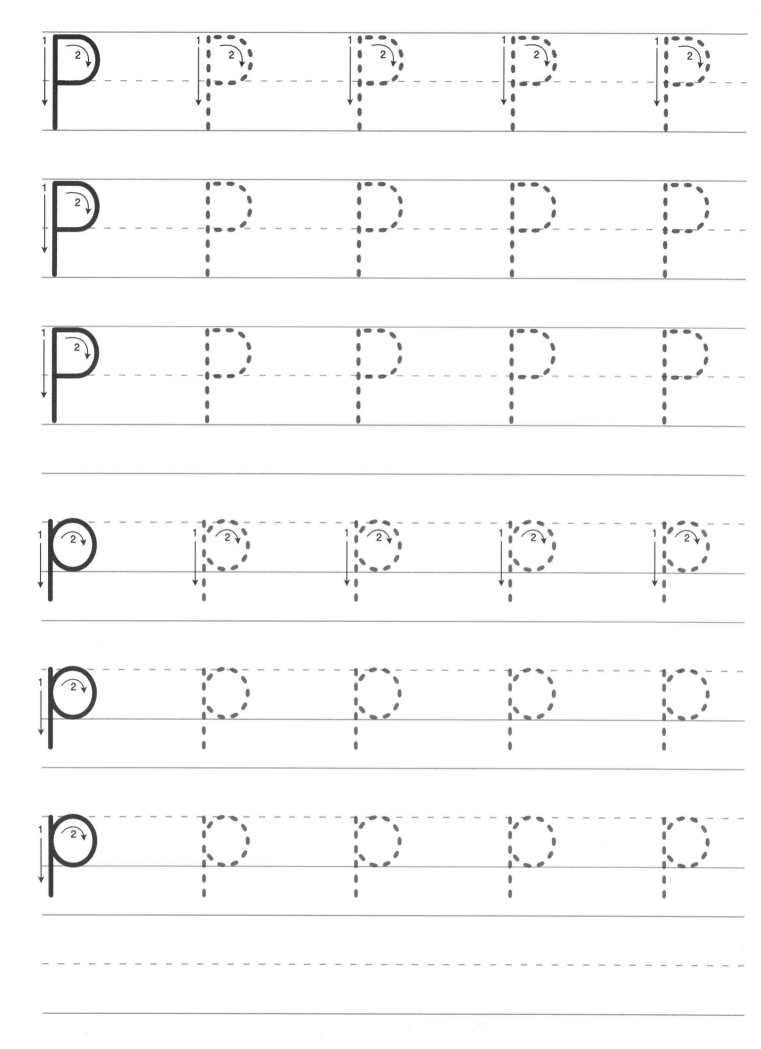

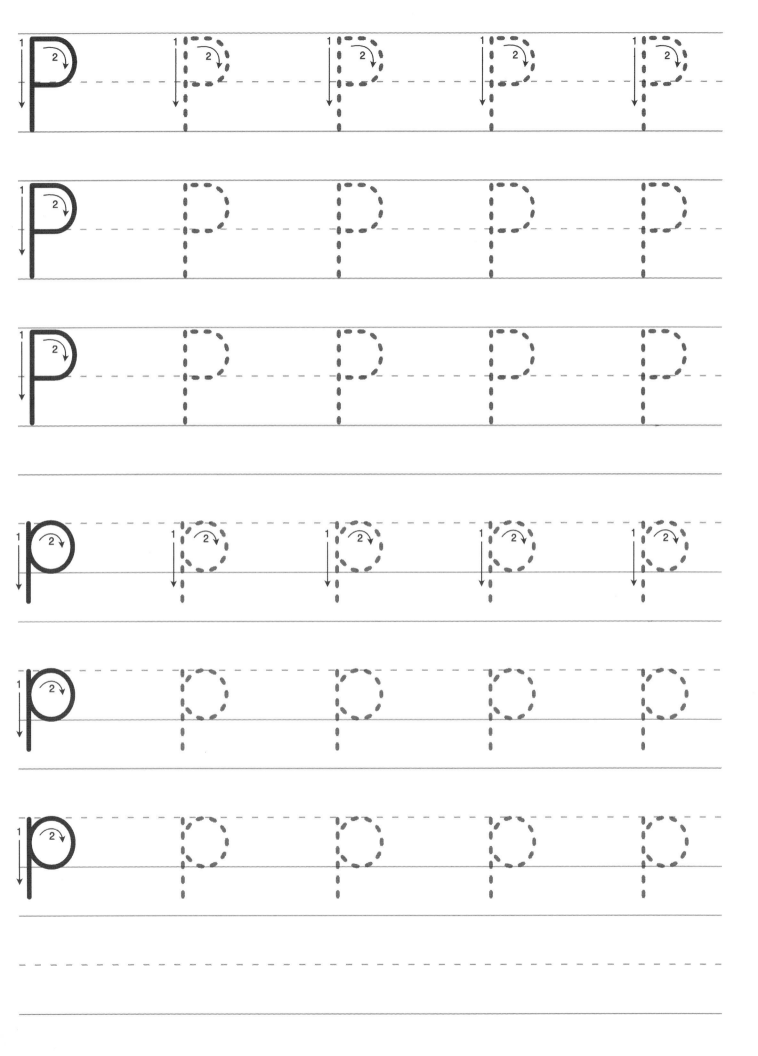

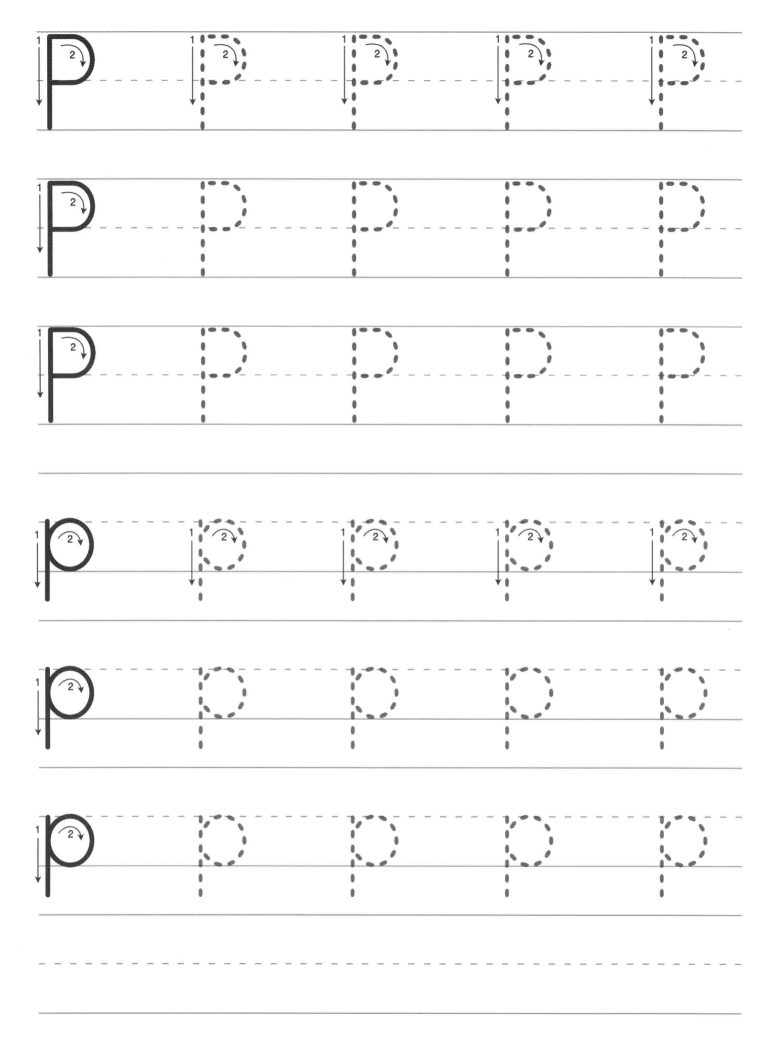

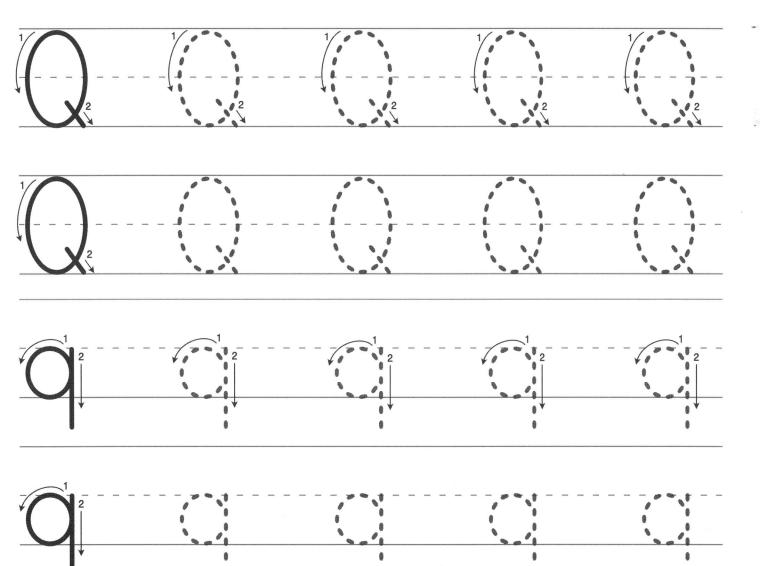

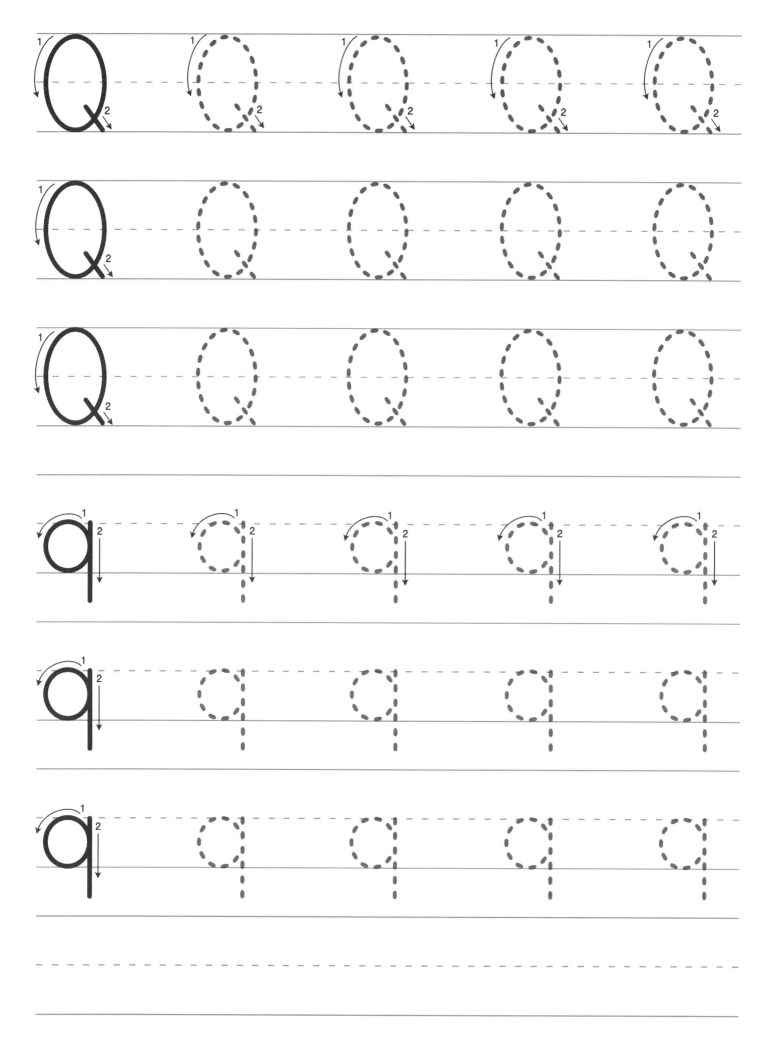

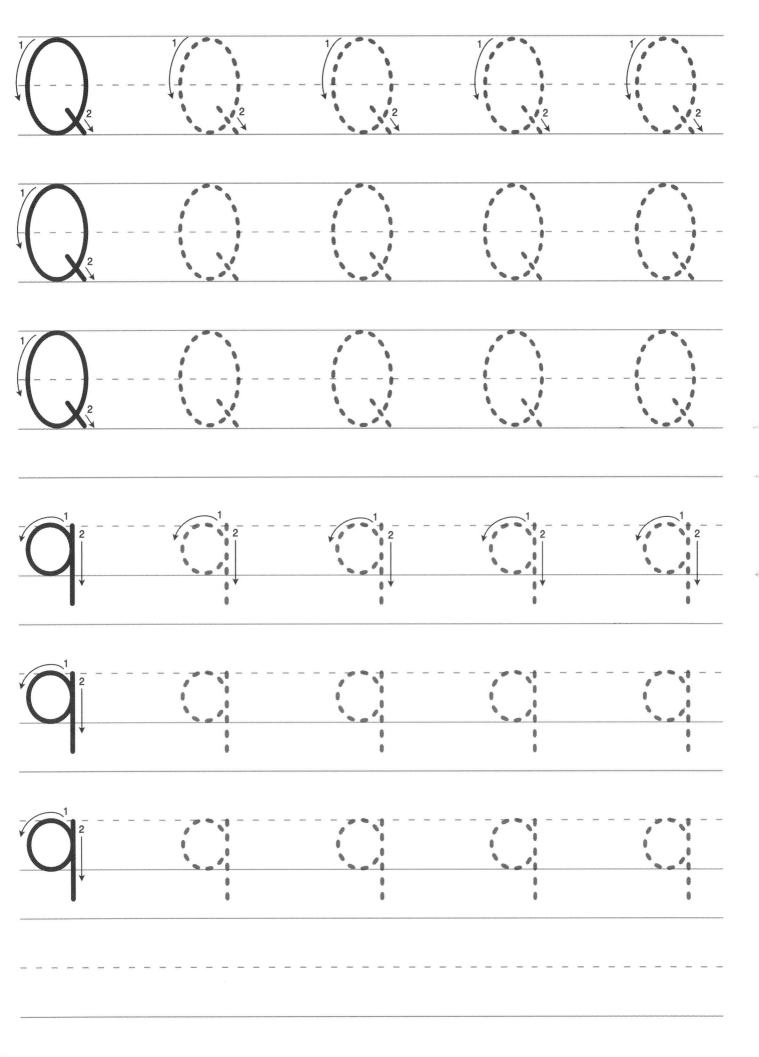

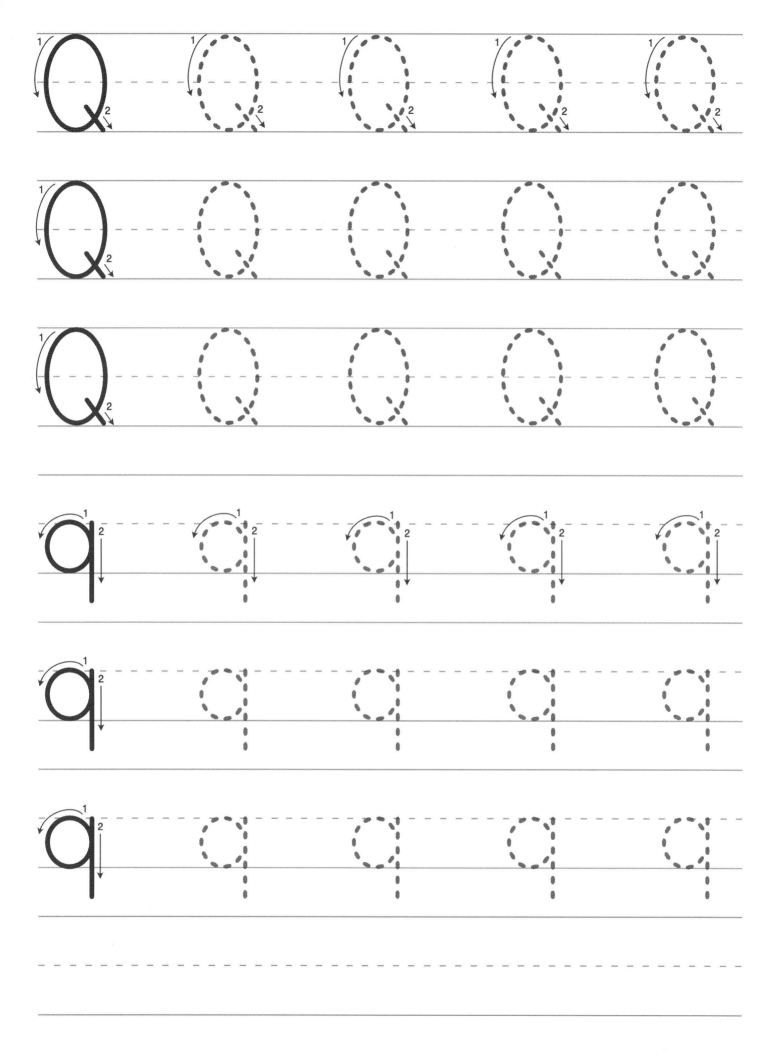

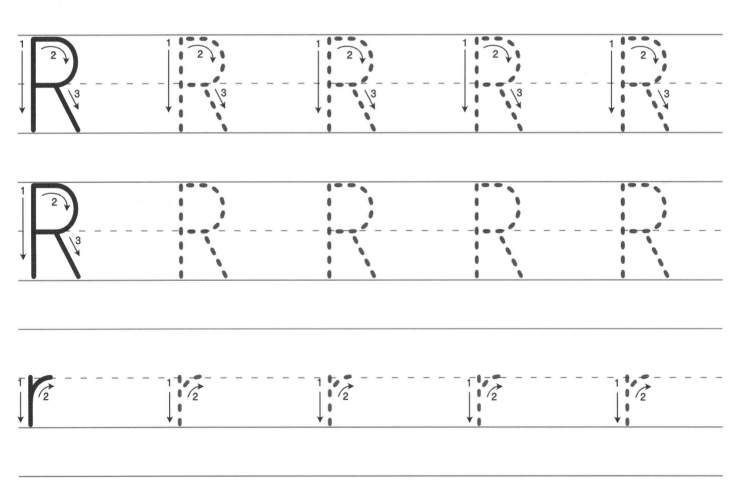

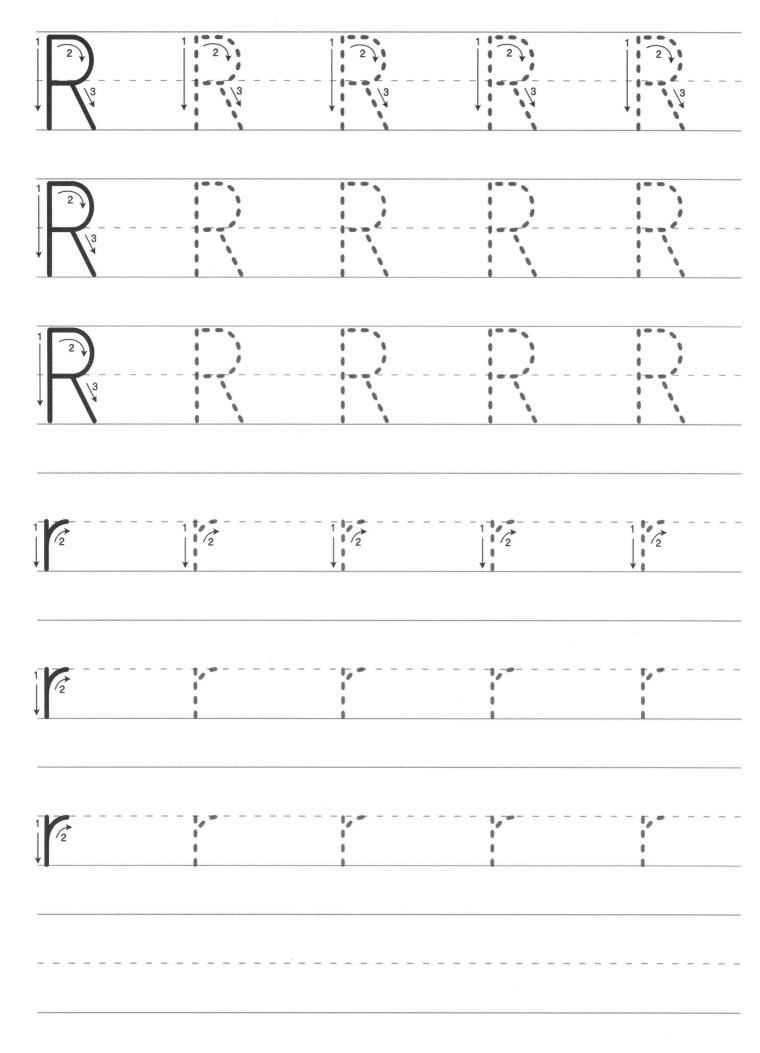

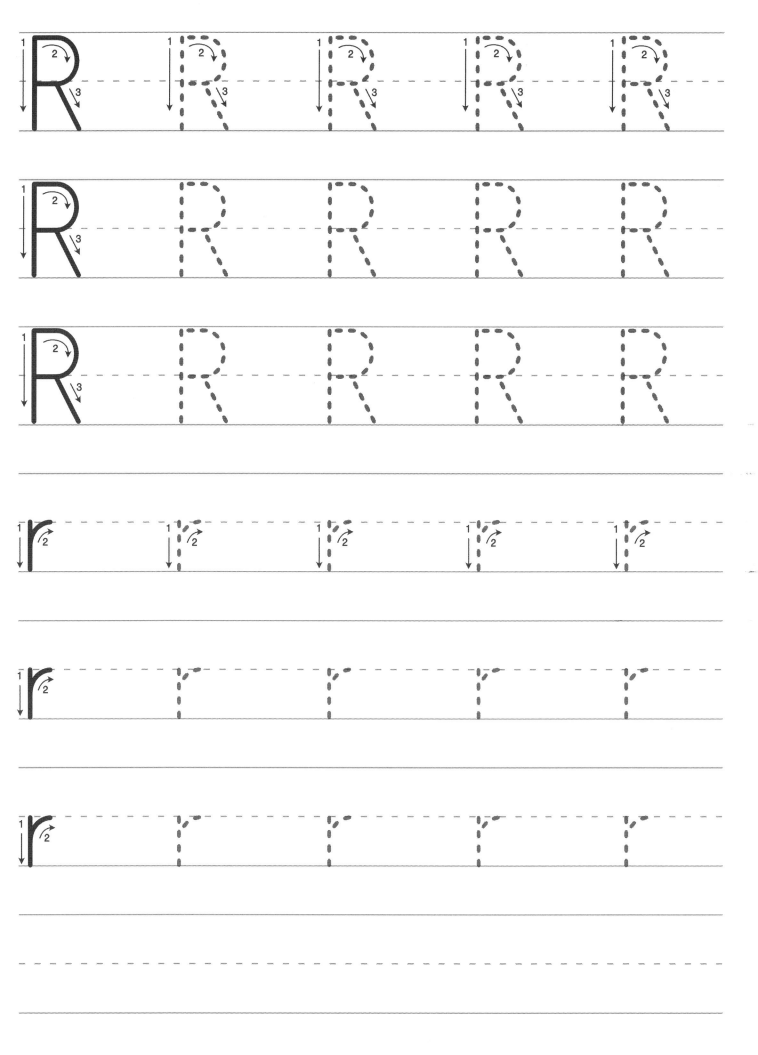

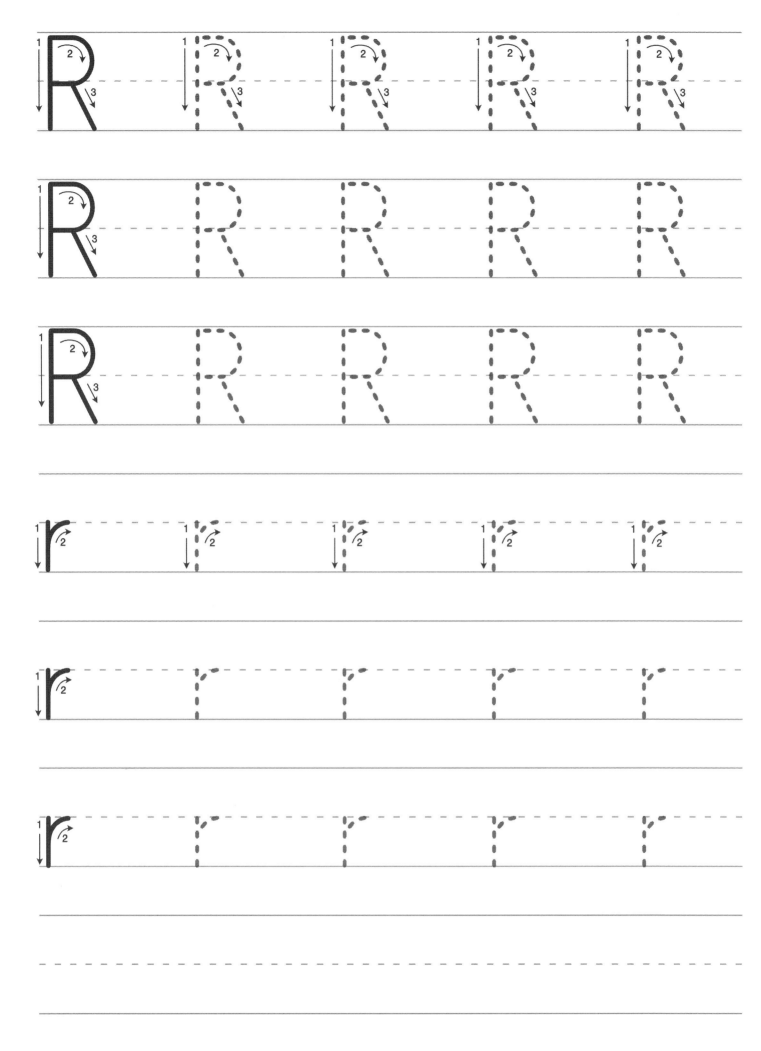

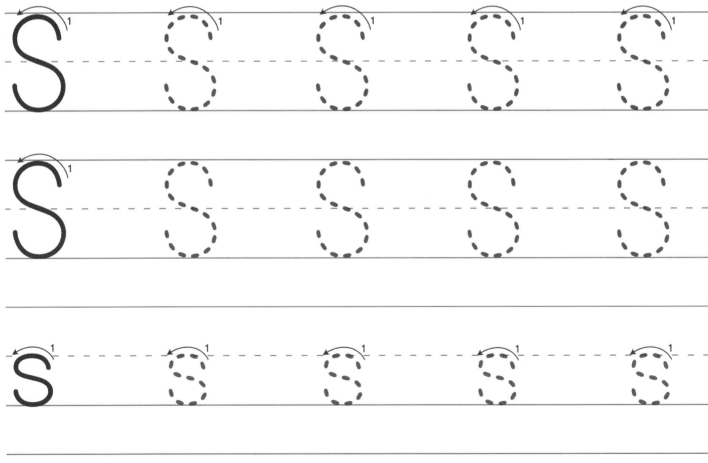

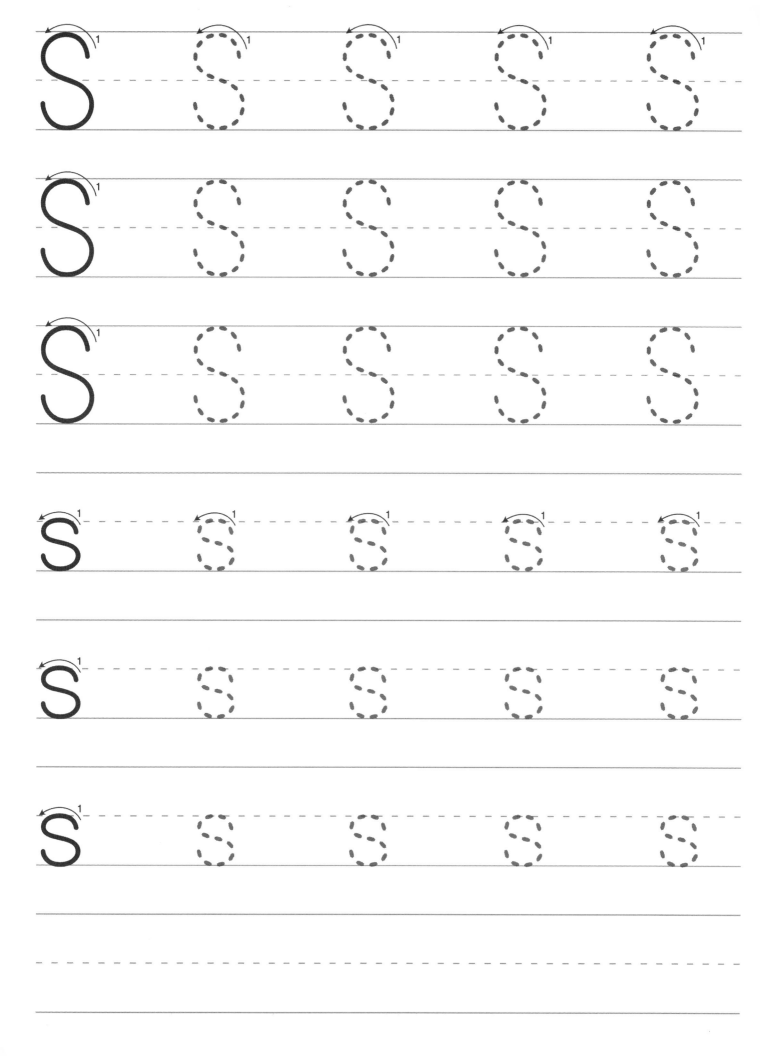

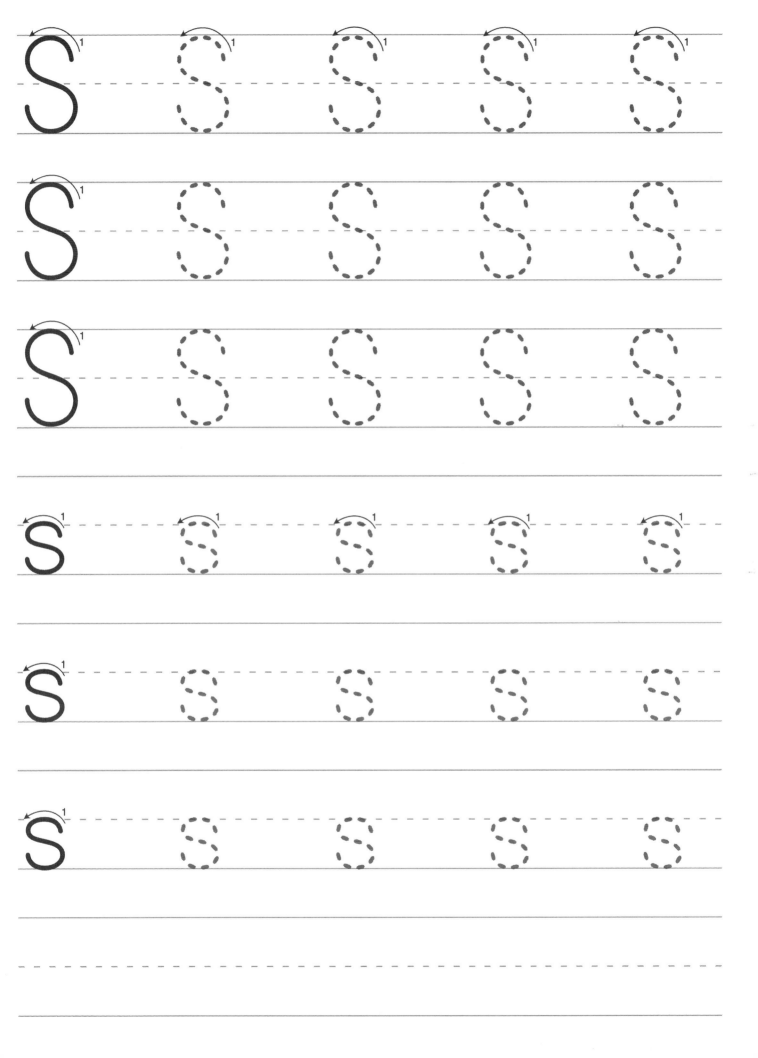

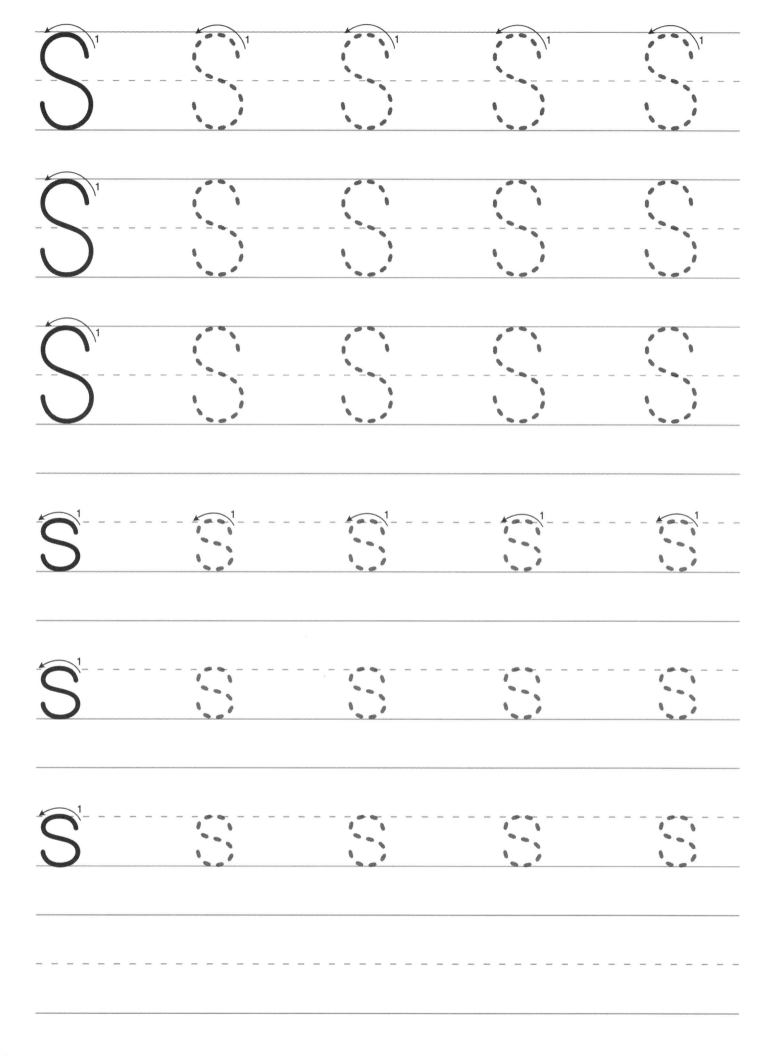

T is for Teddy

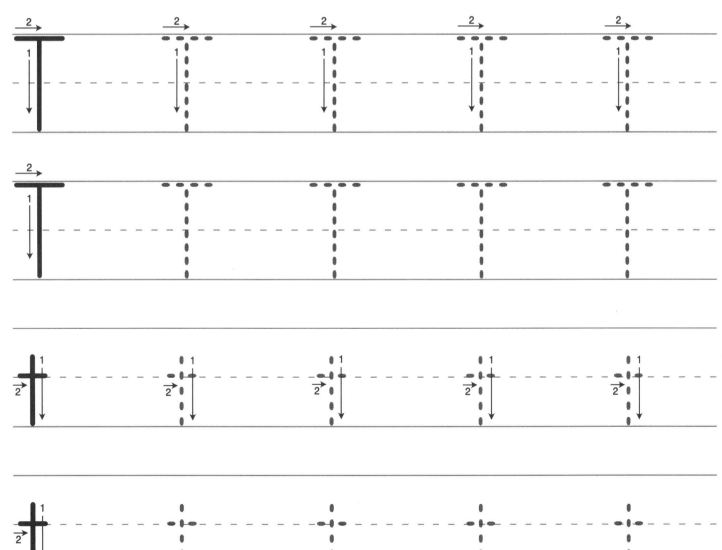

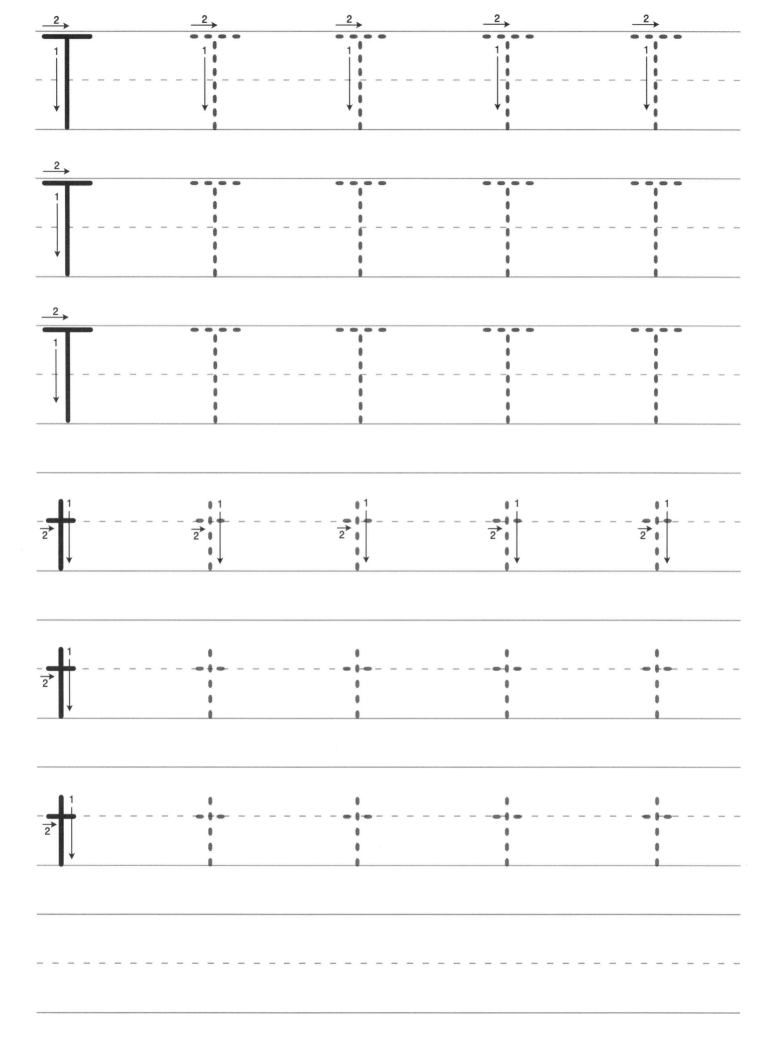

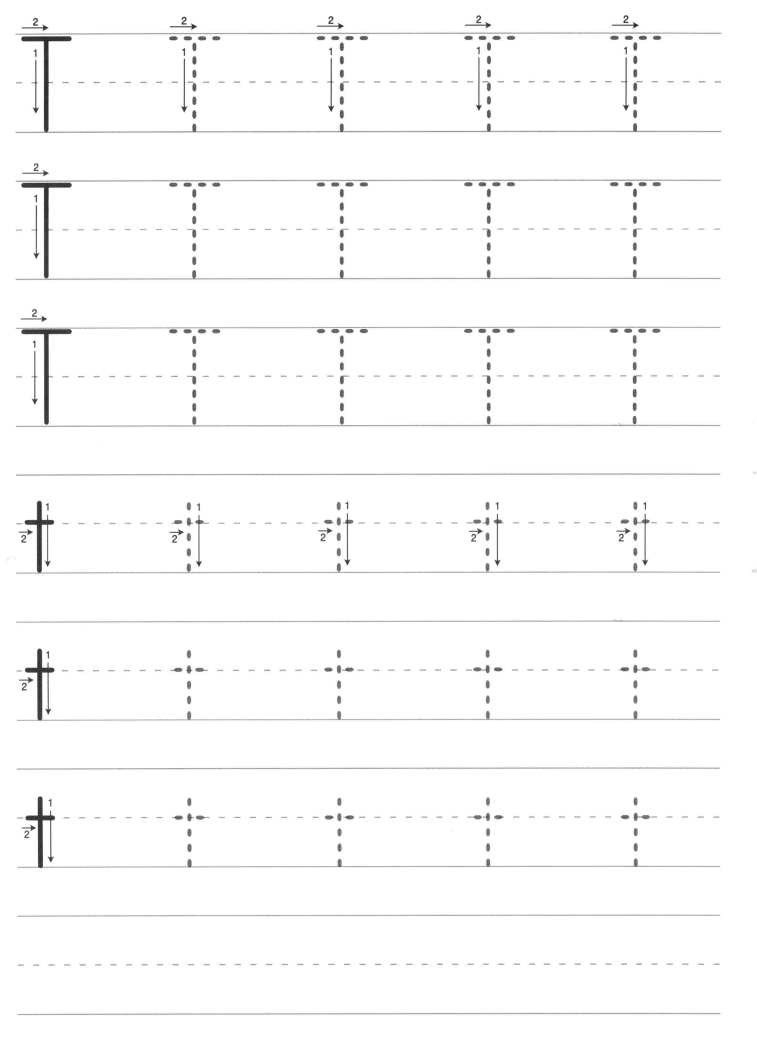

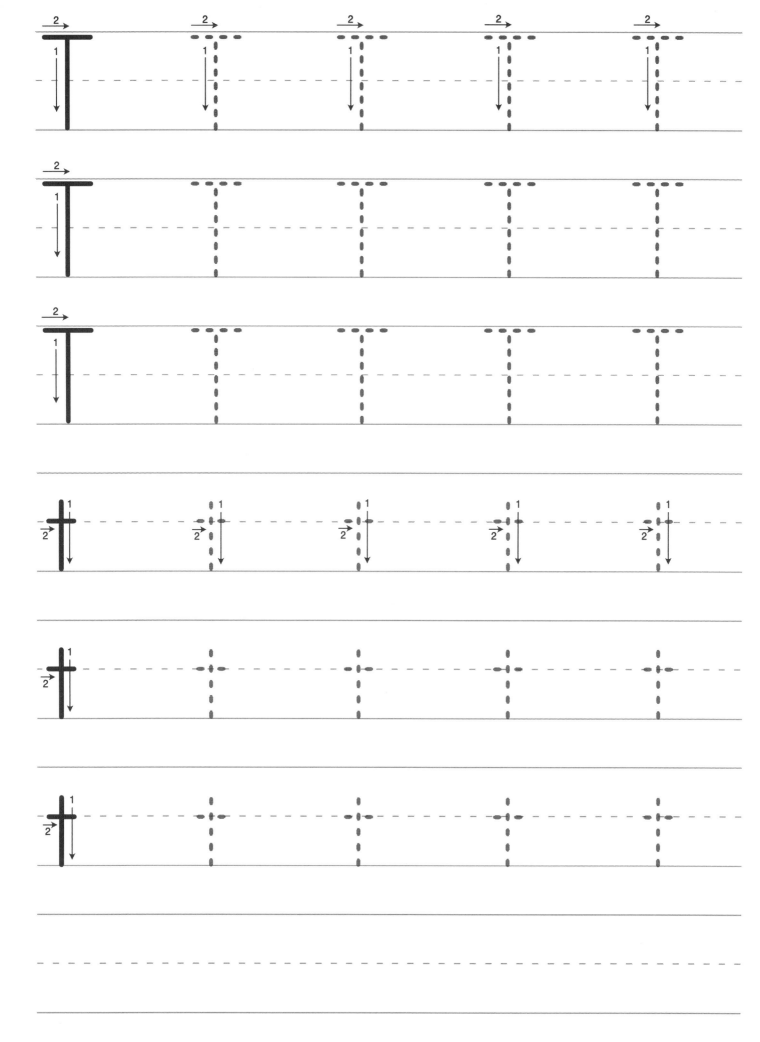

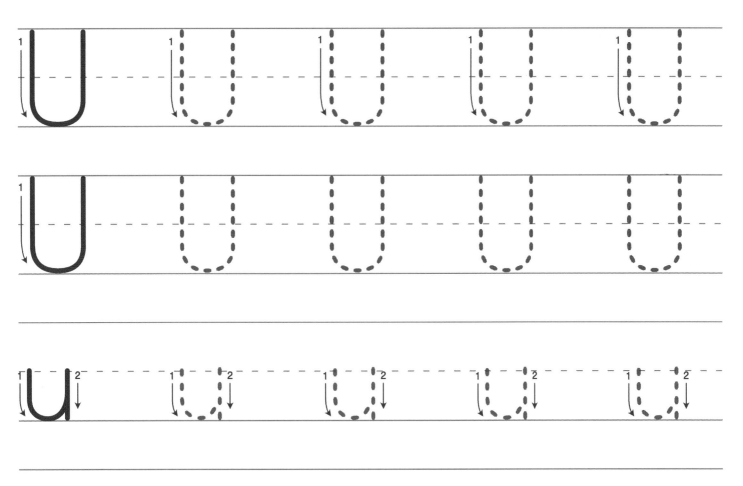

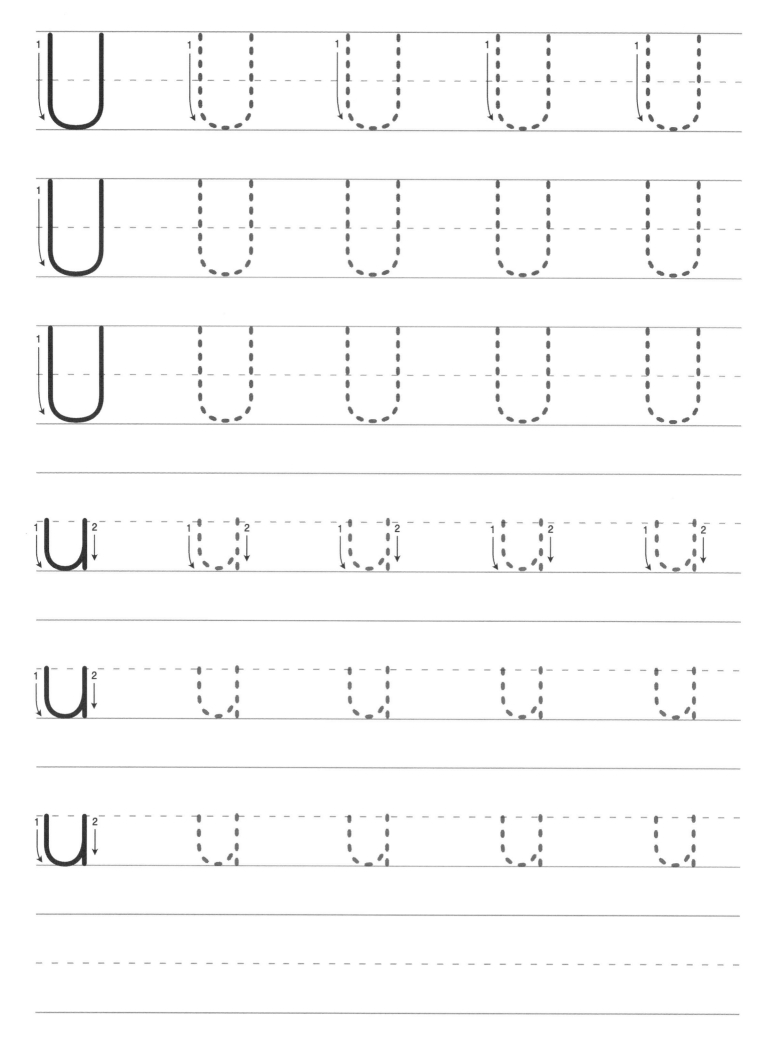

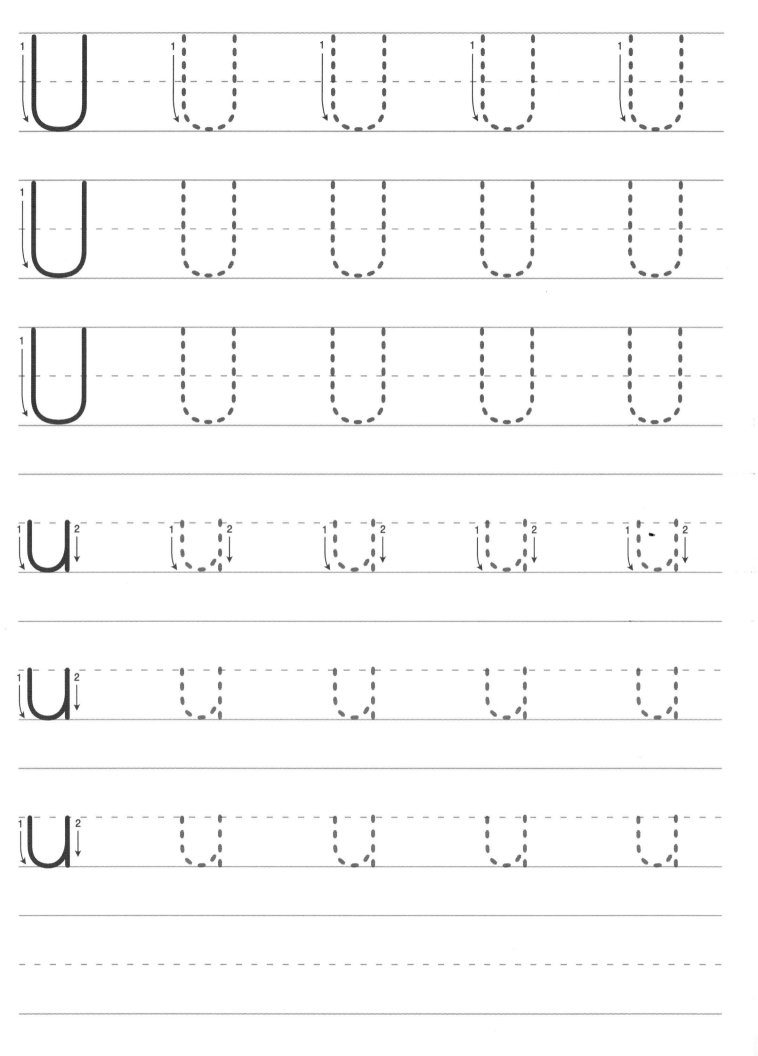

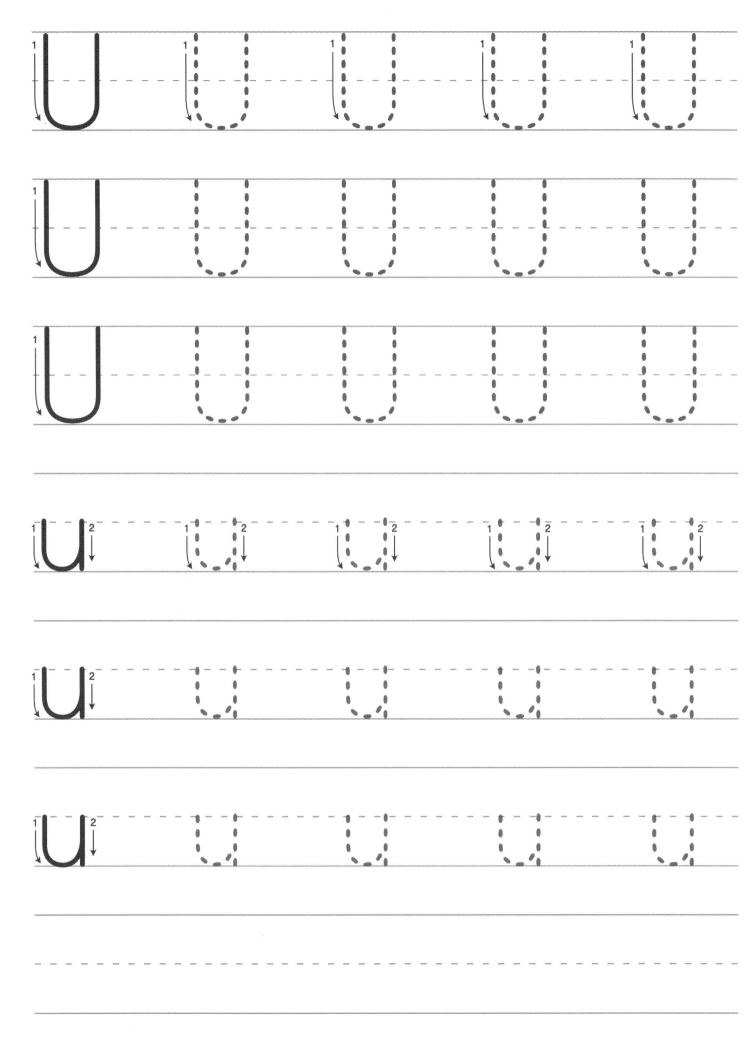

V is for Van

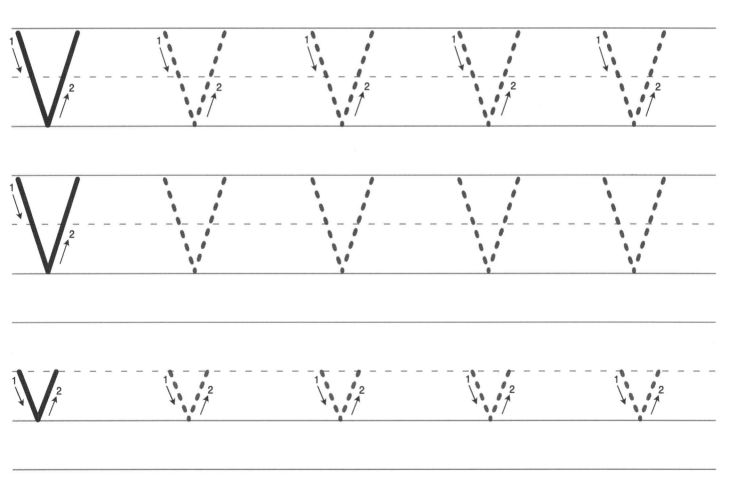

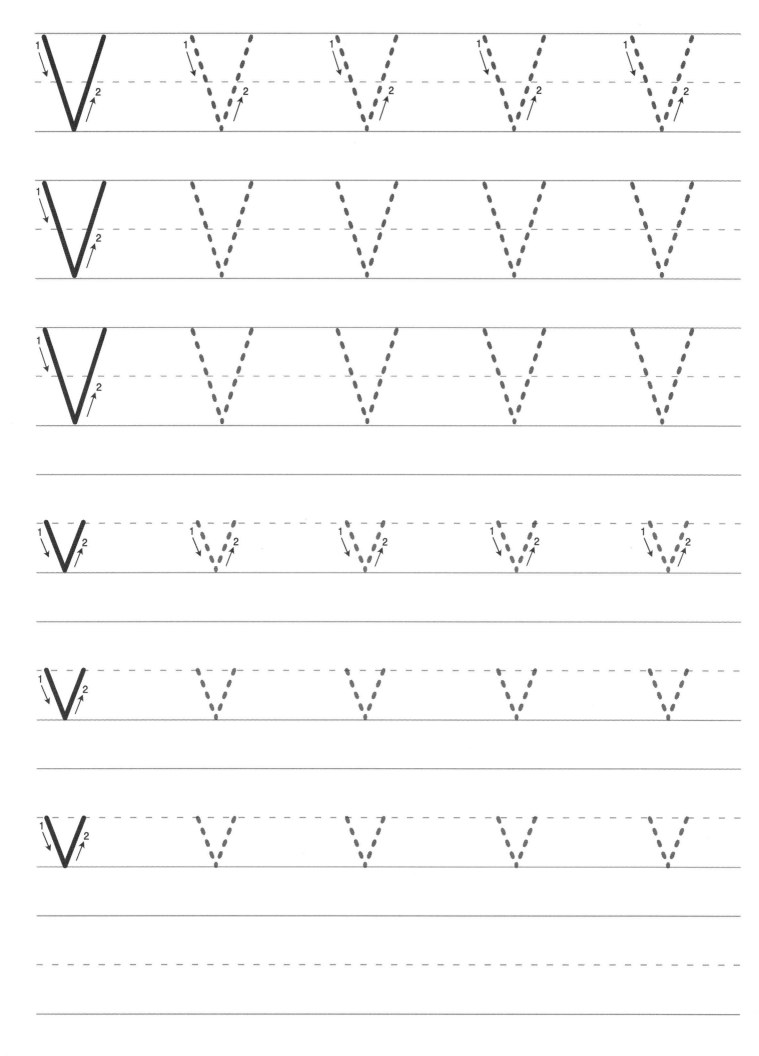

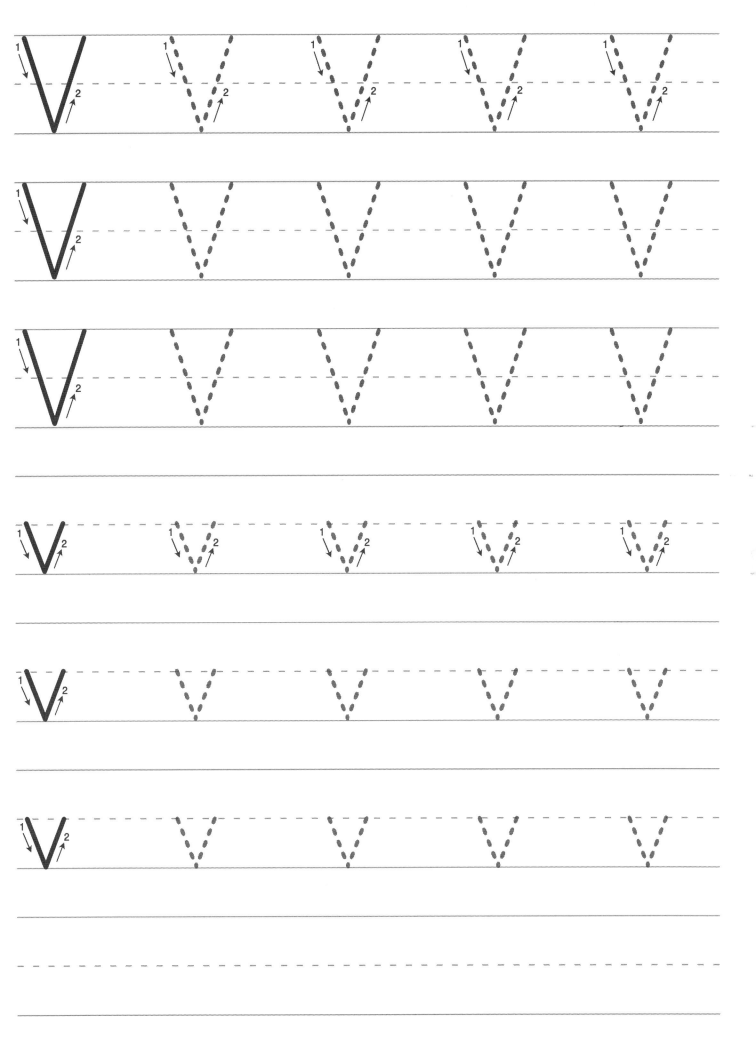

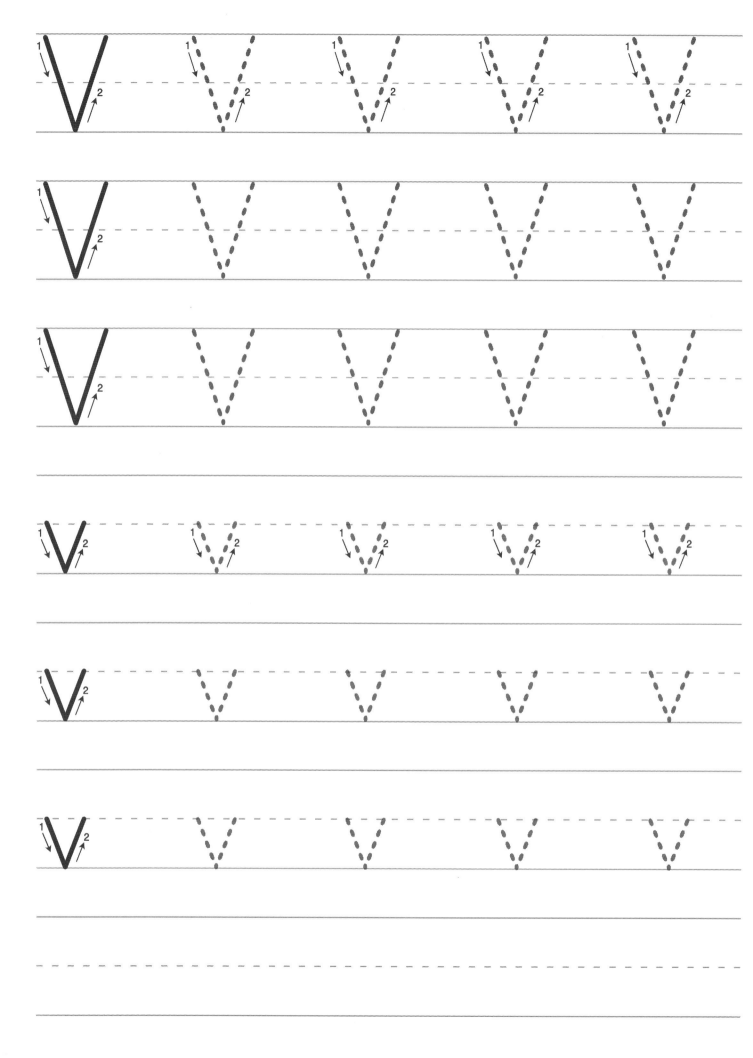

W is for Whale

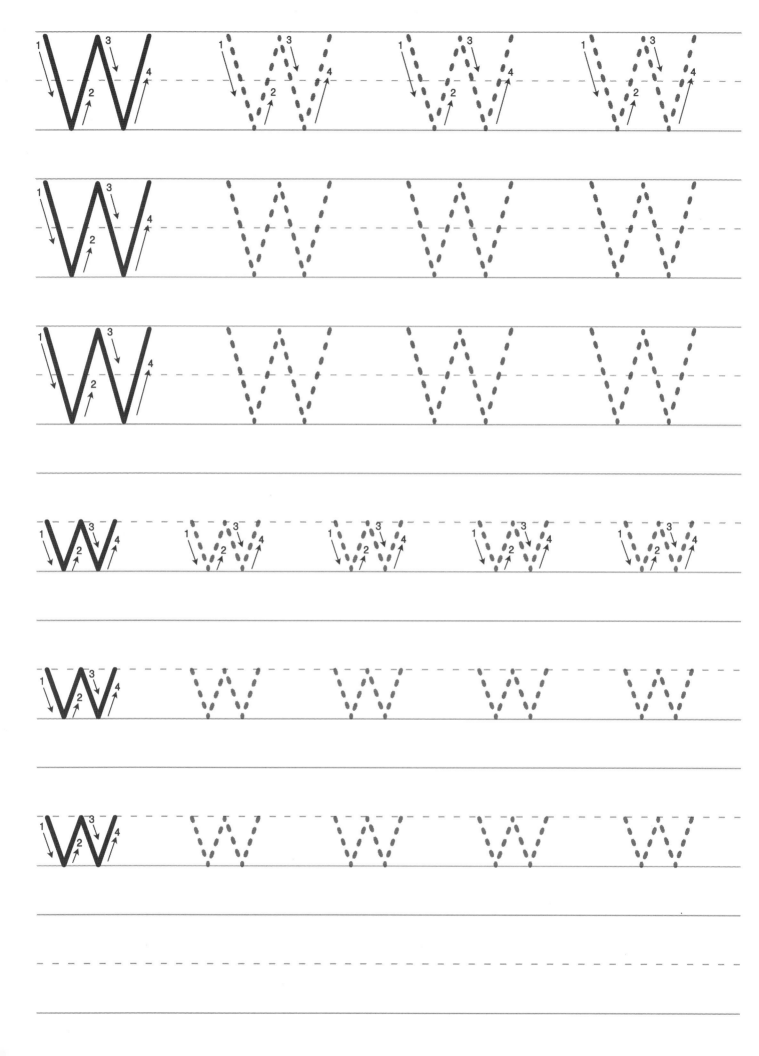

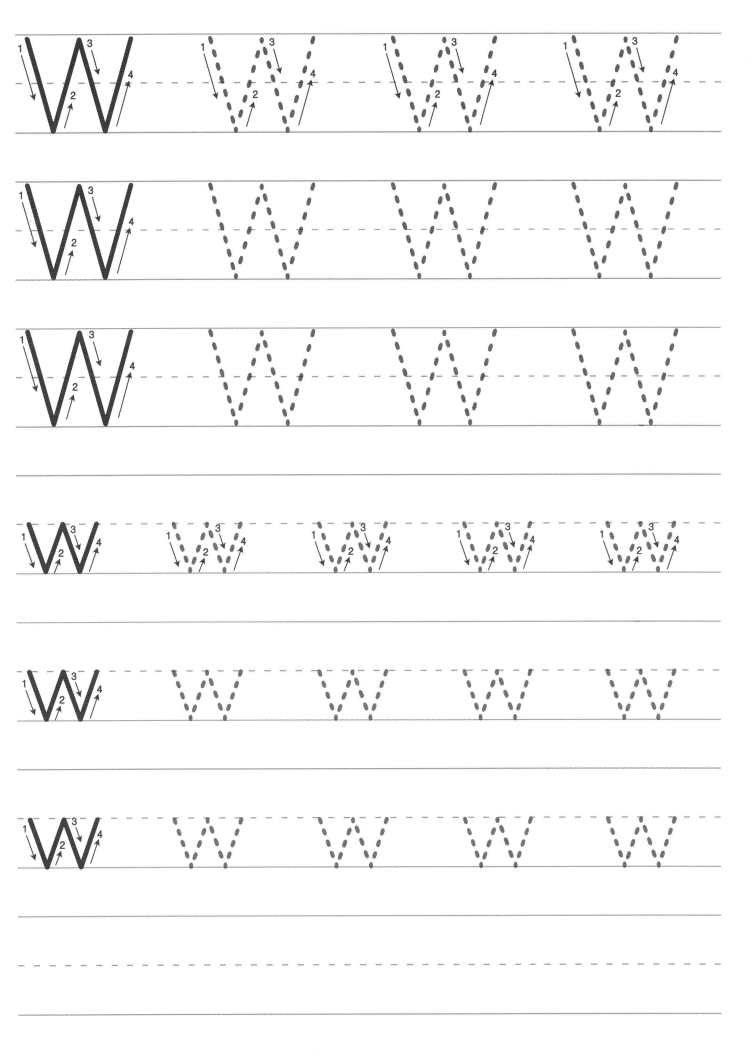

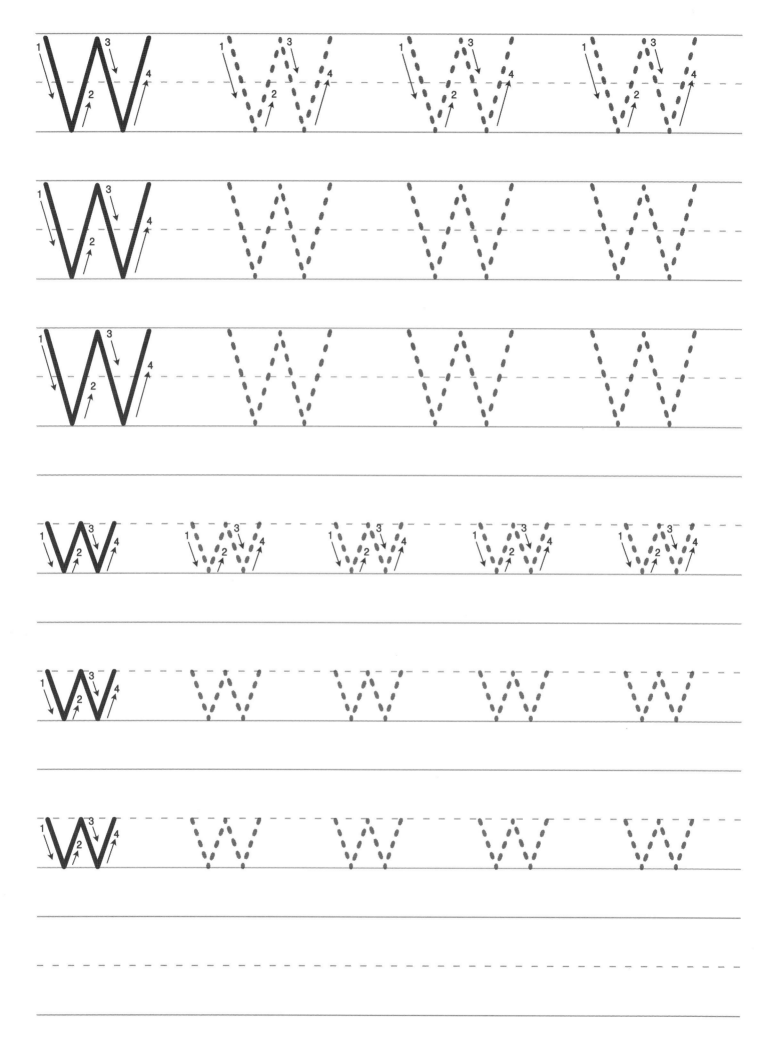

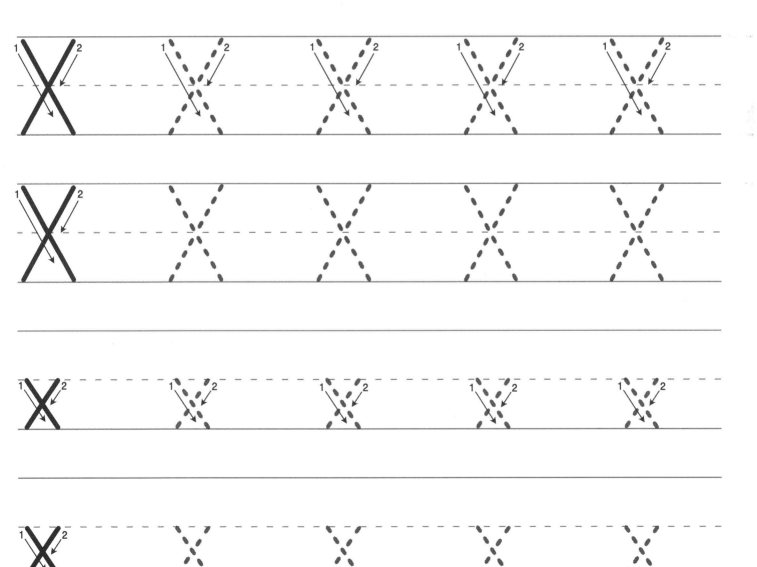

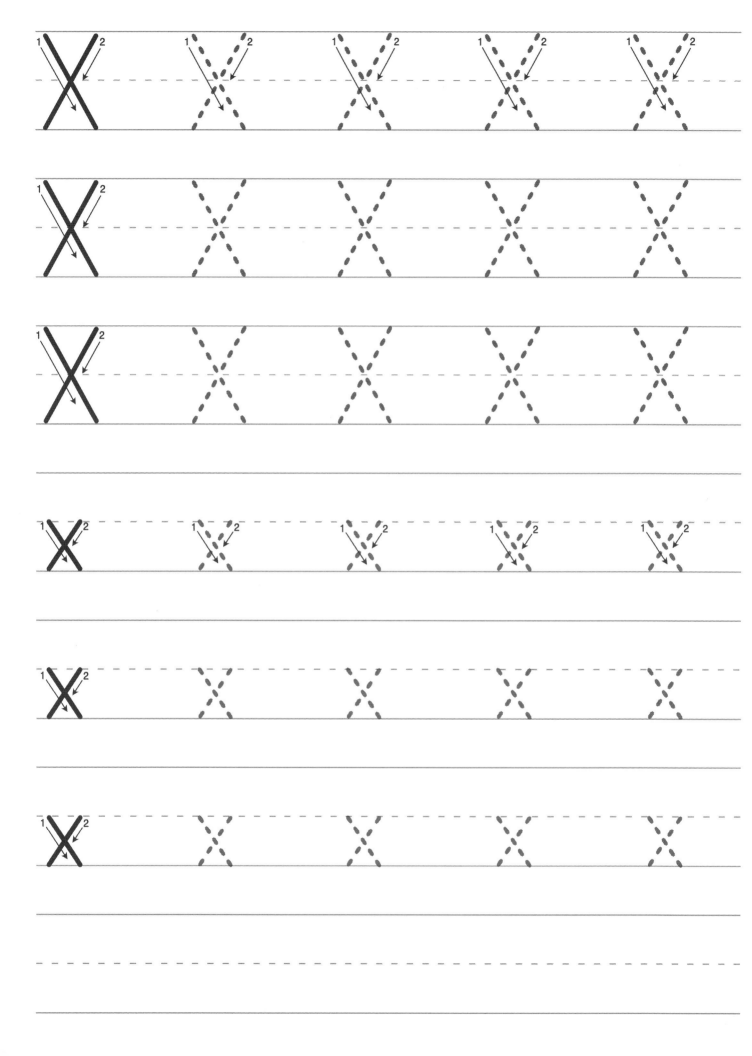

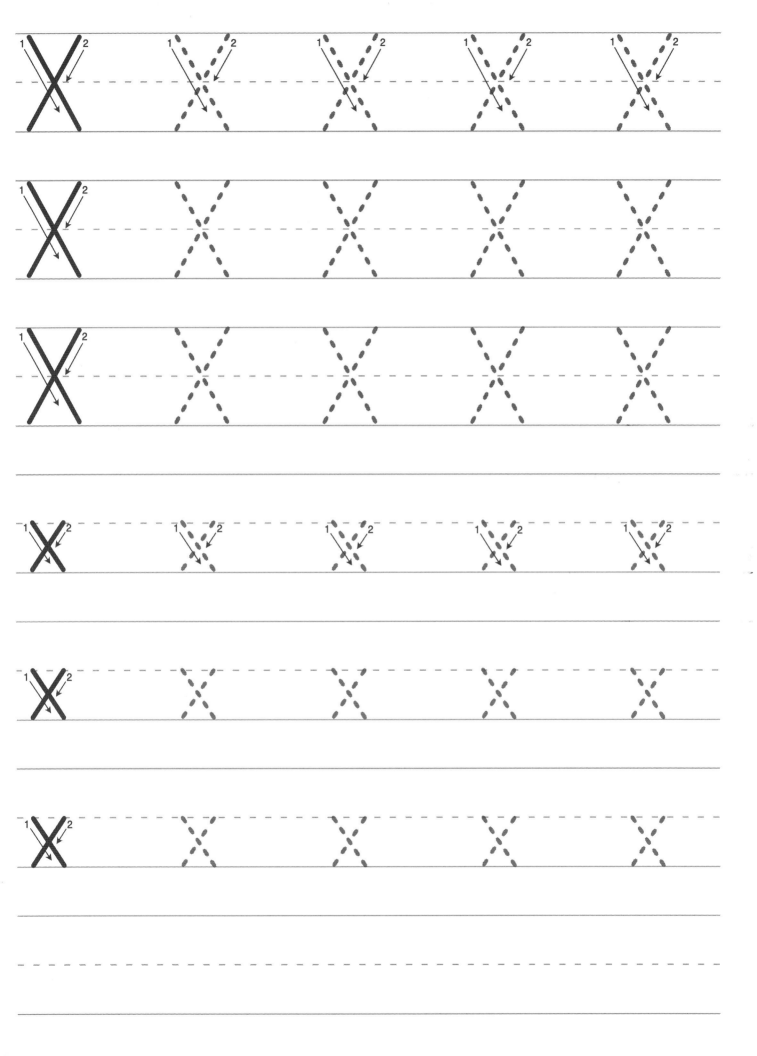

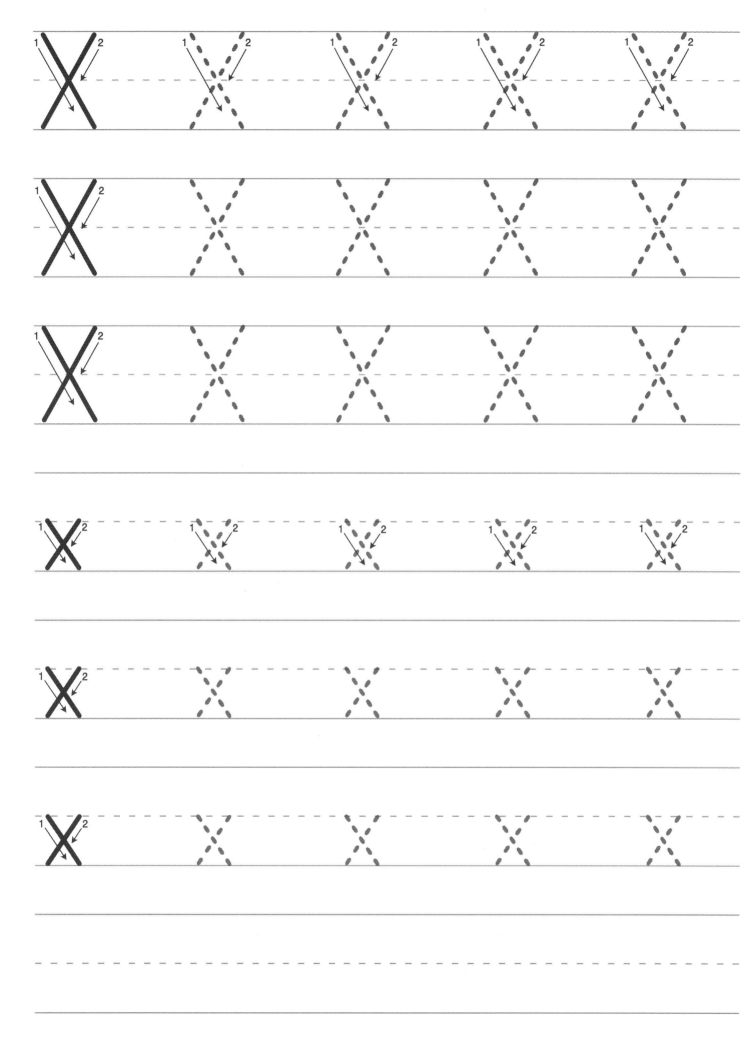

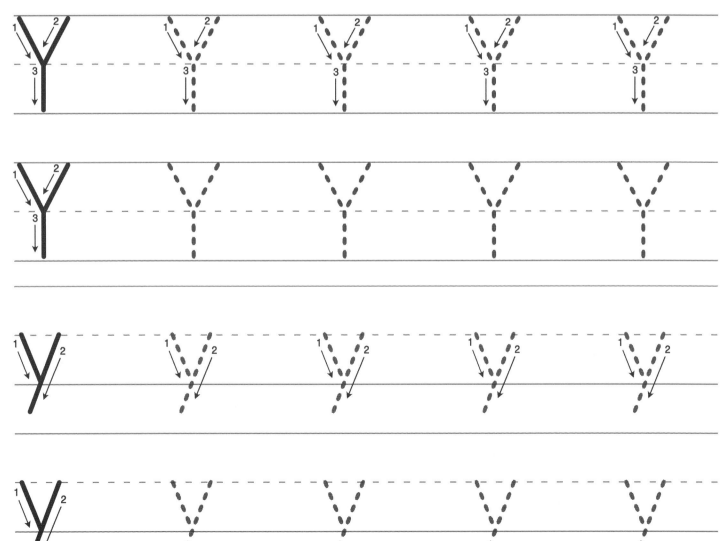

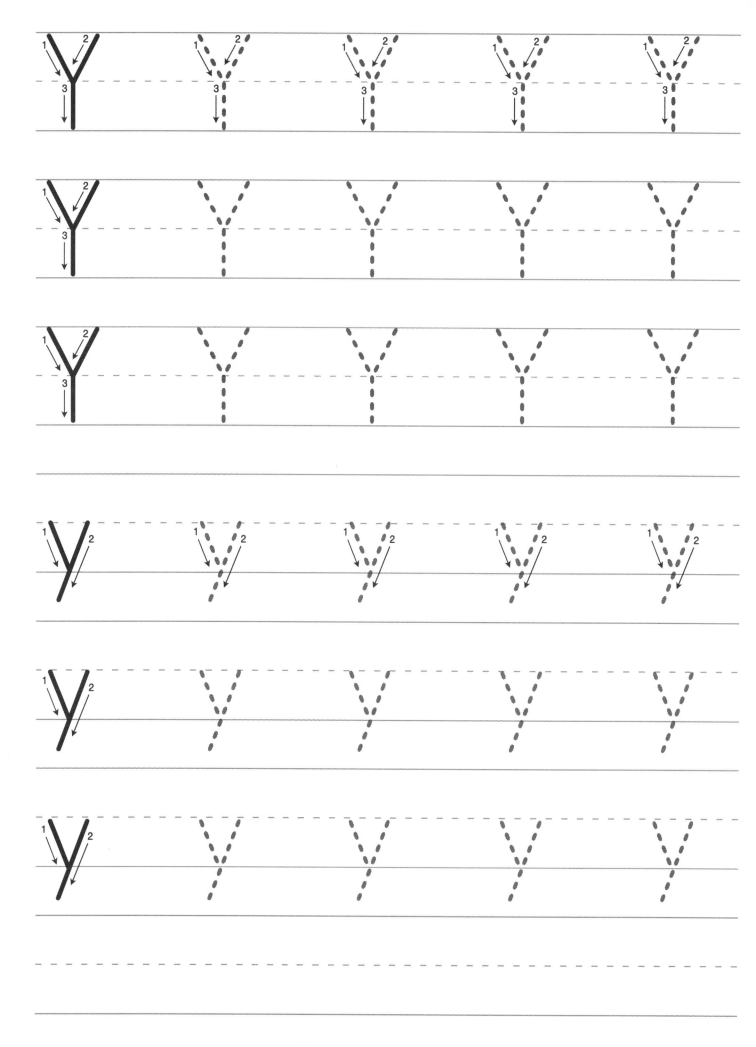

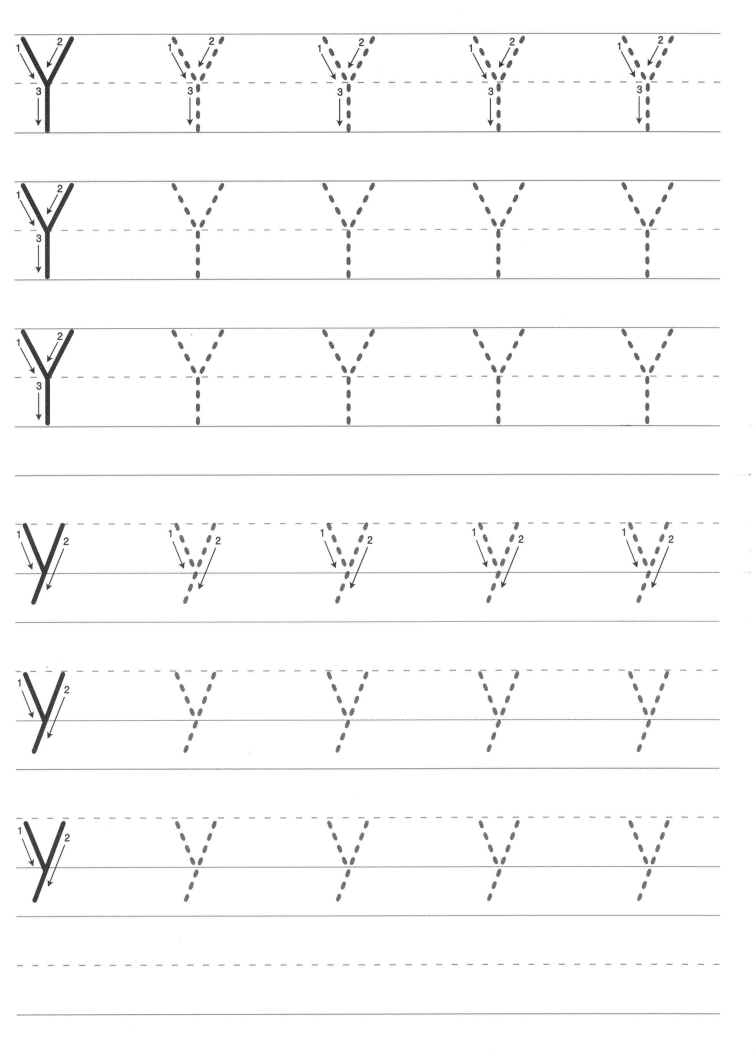

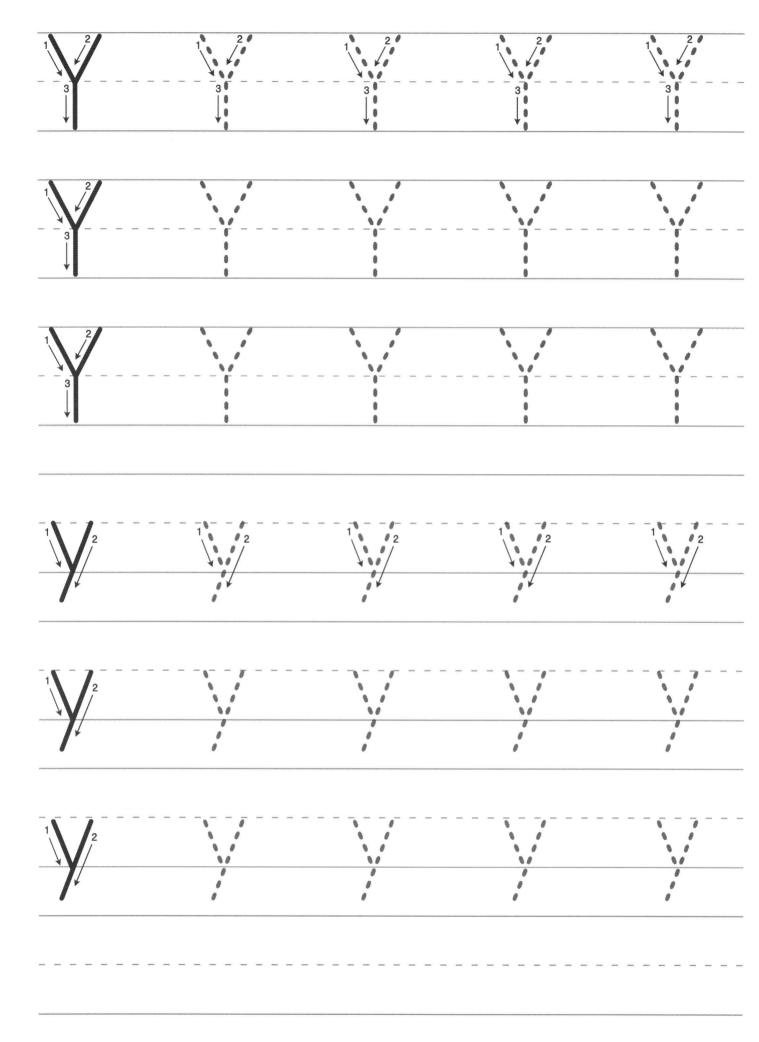

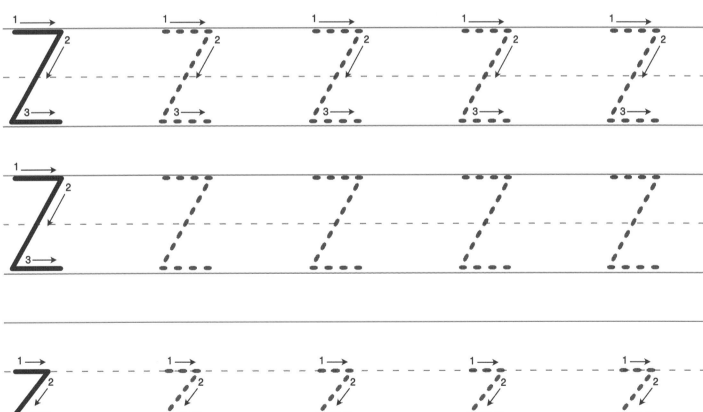

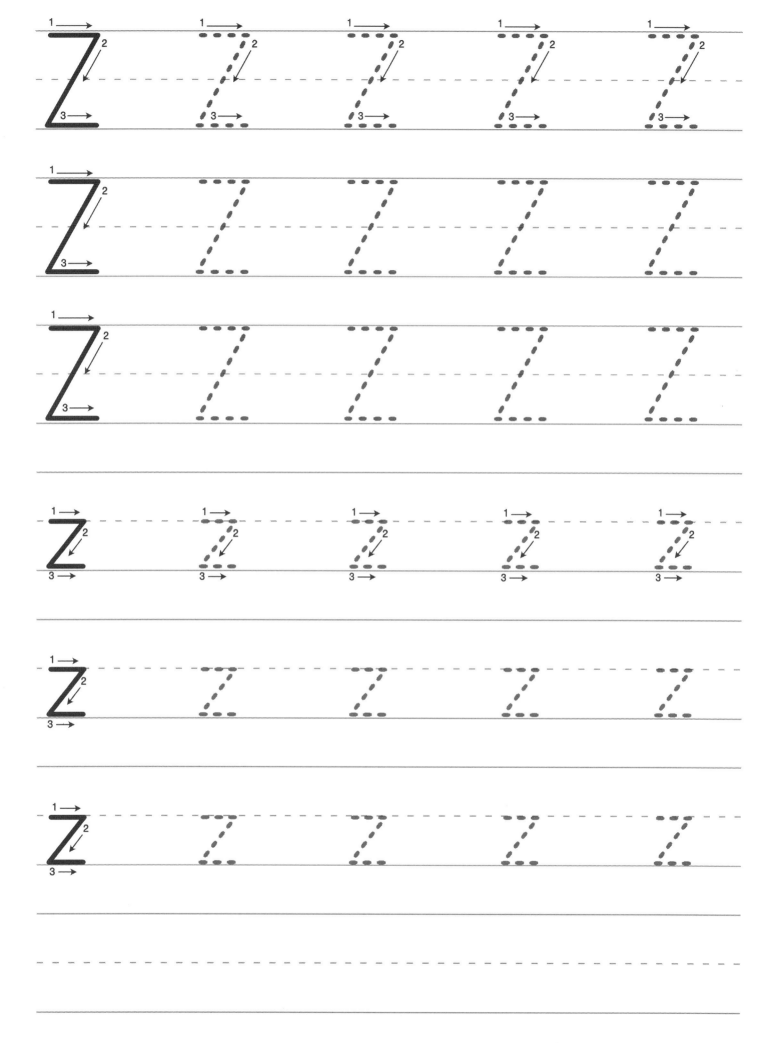

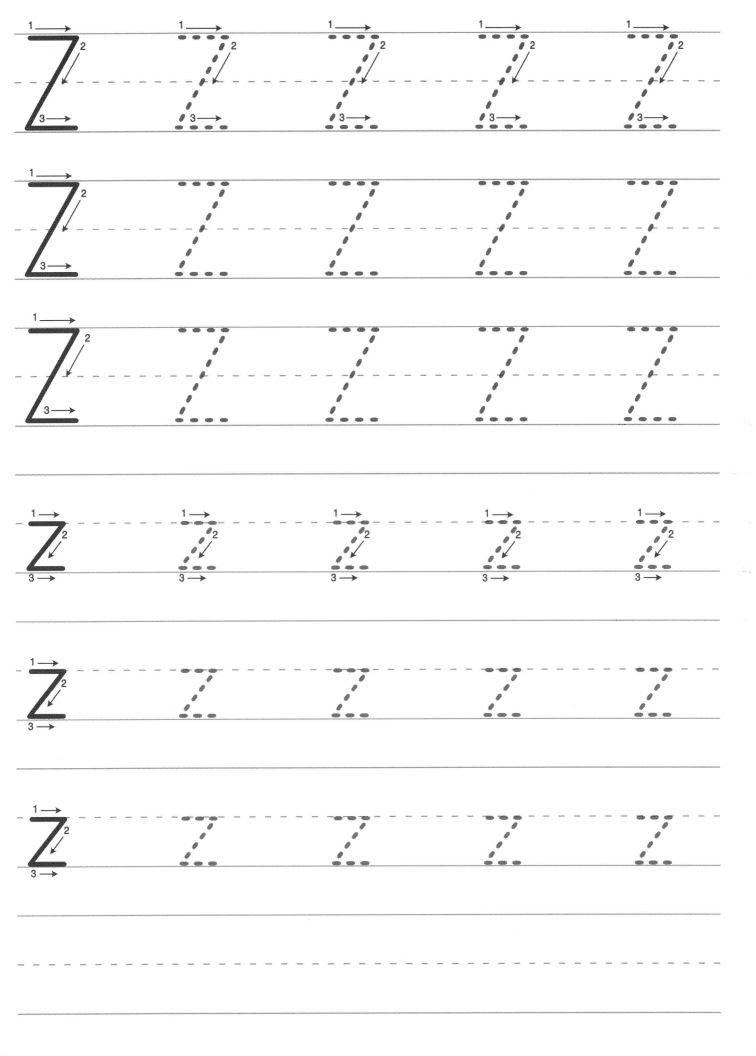

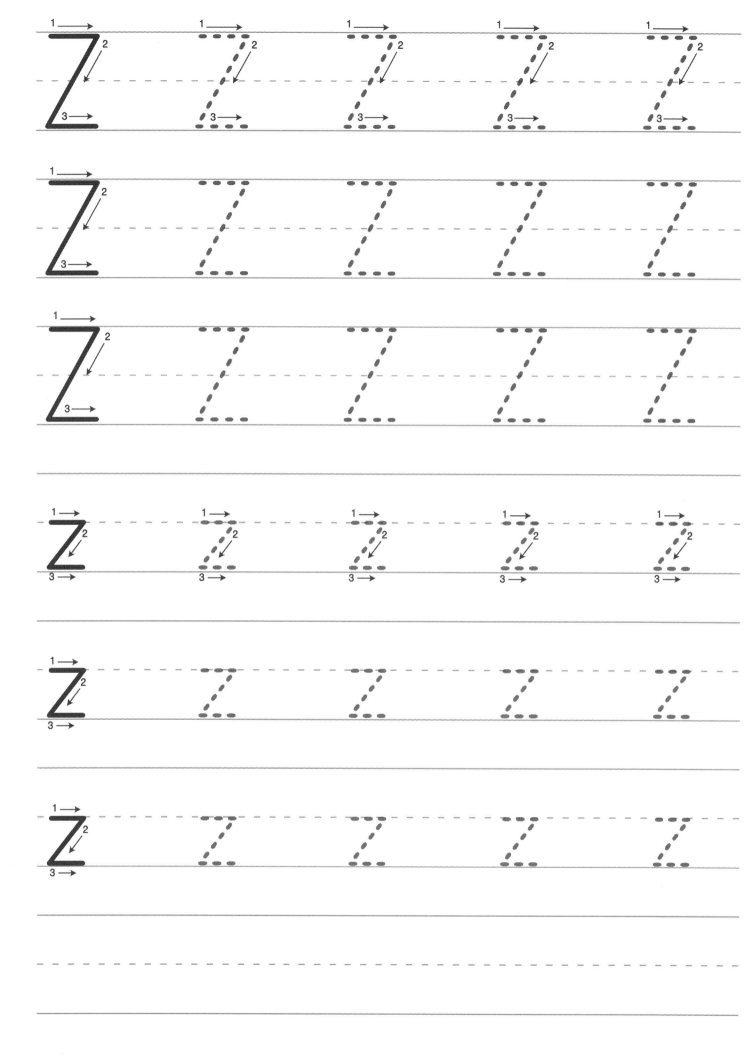

Below you can write down some letters.

Section 2:

Trace the numbers and color in the pictures.

Two Turtles

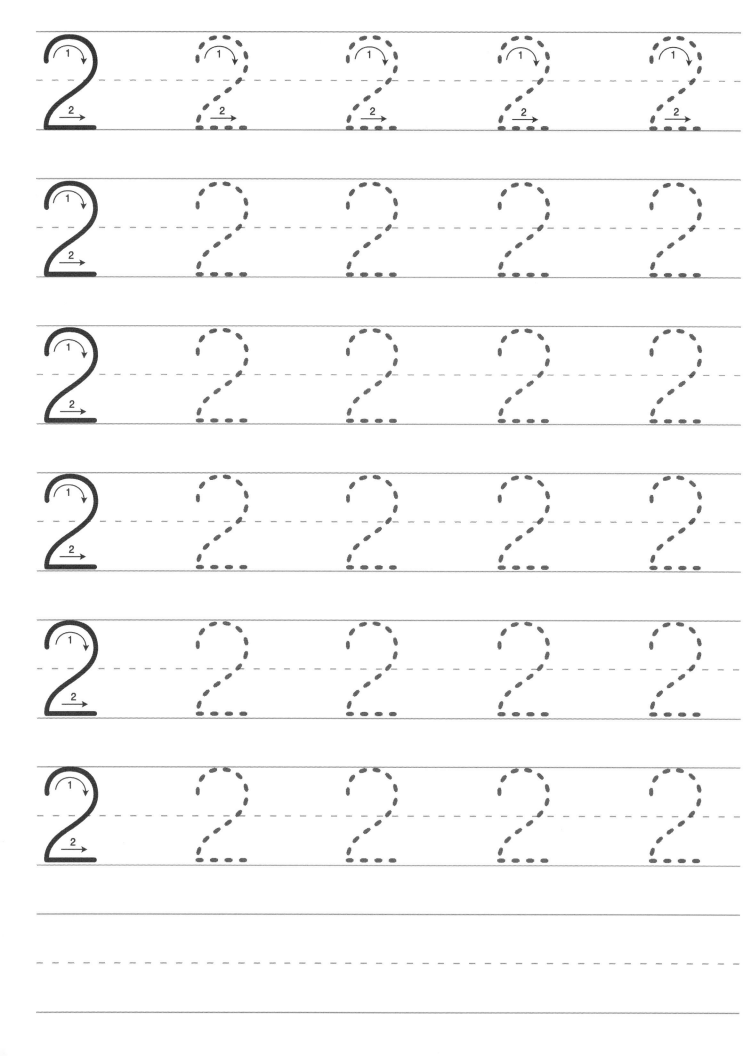

3 Three Butterflies

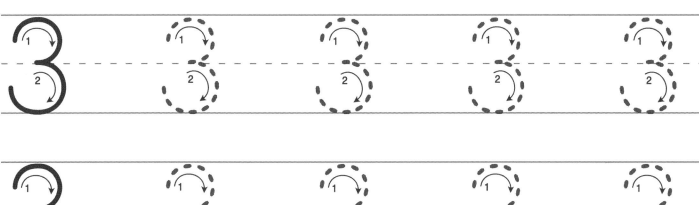
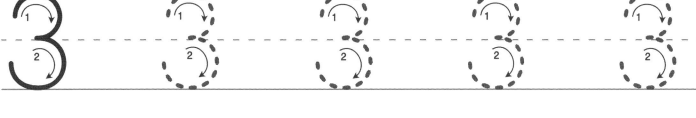
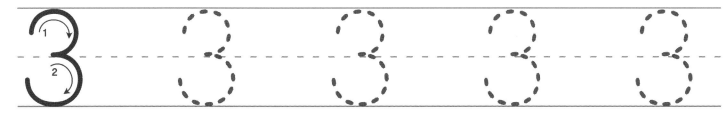
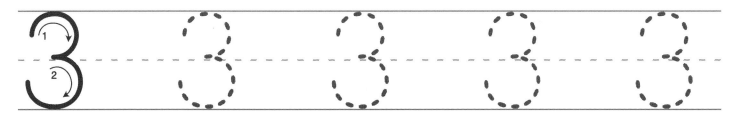

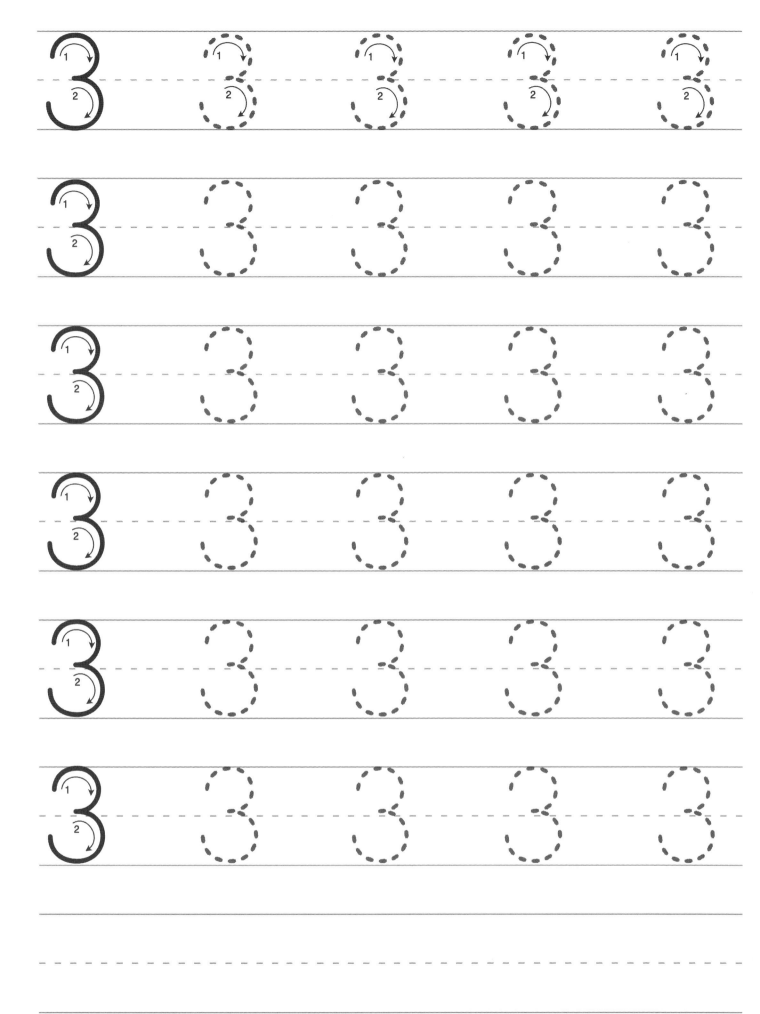

Four Fish

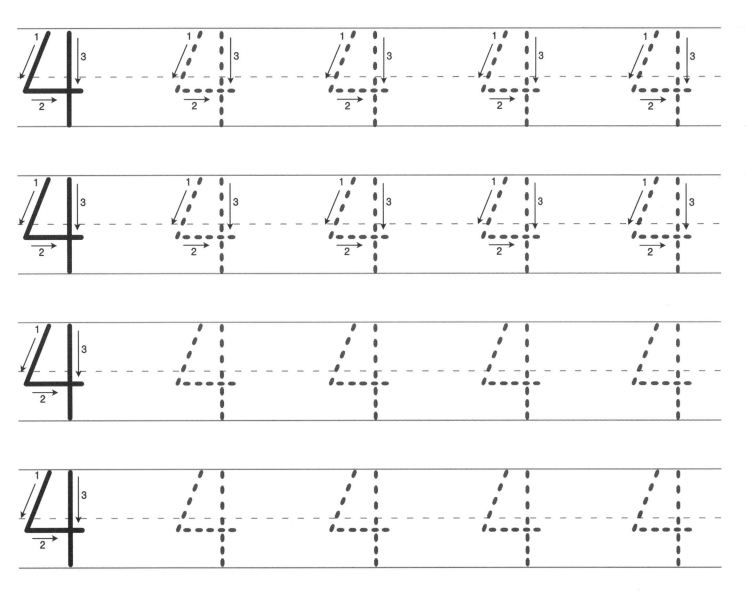

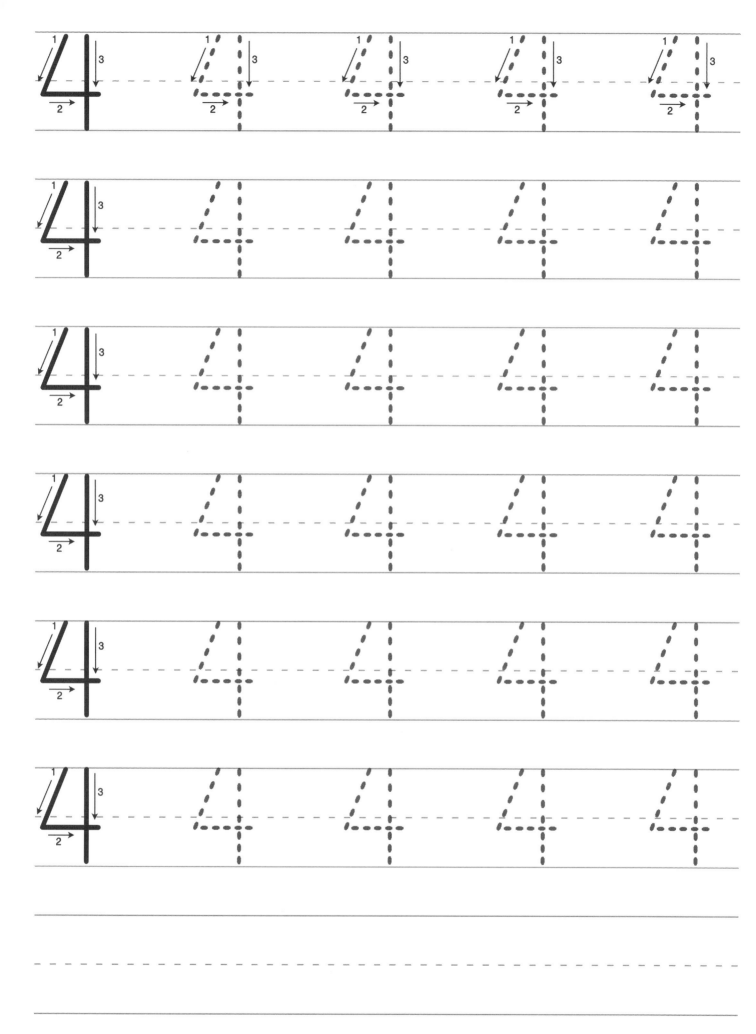

5 Five Fruits

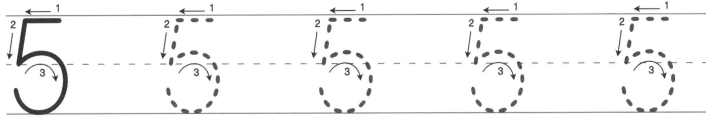
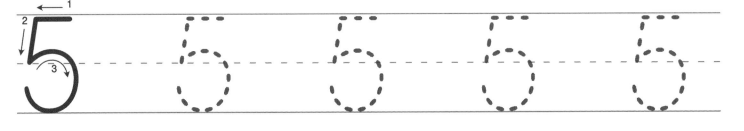
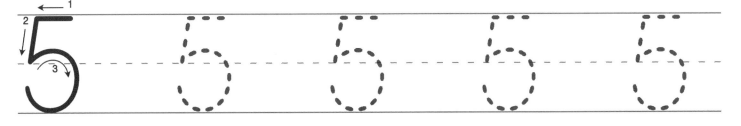

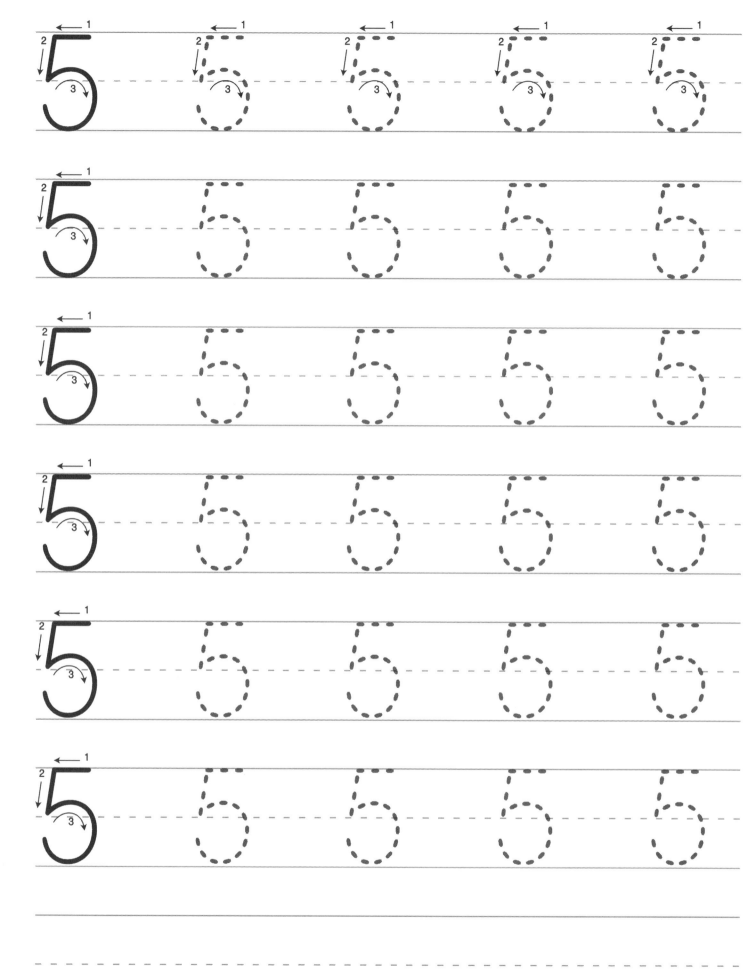

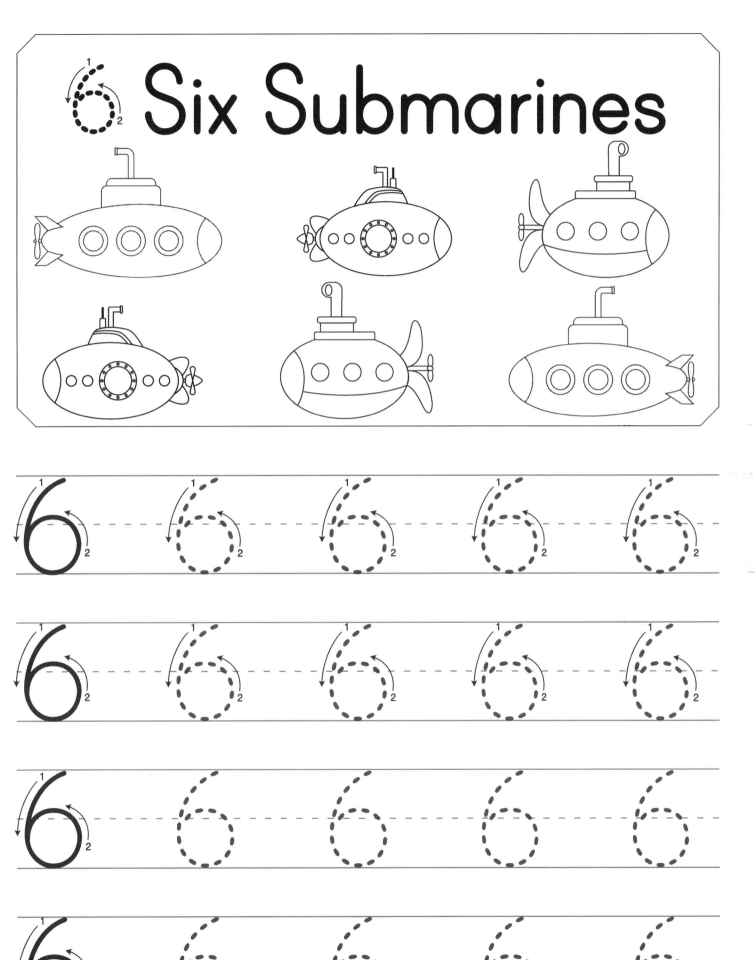

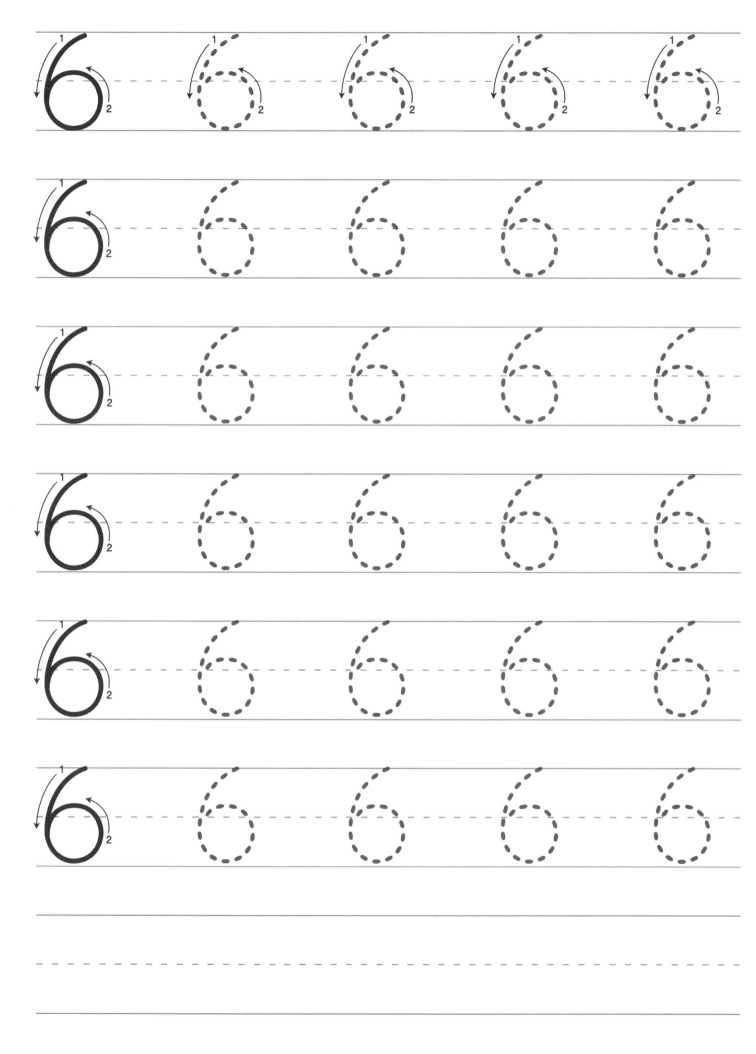

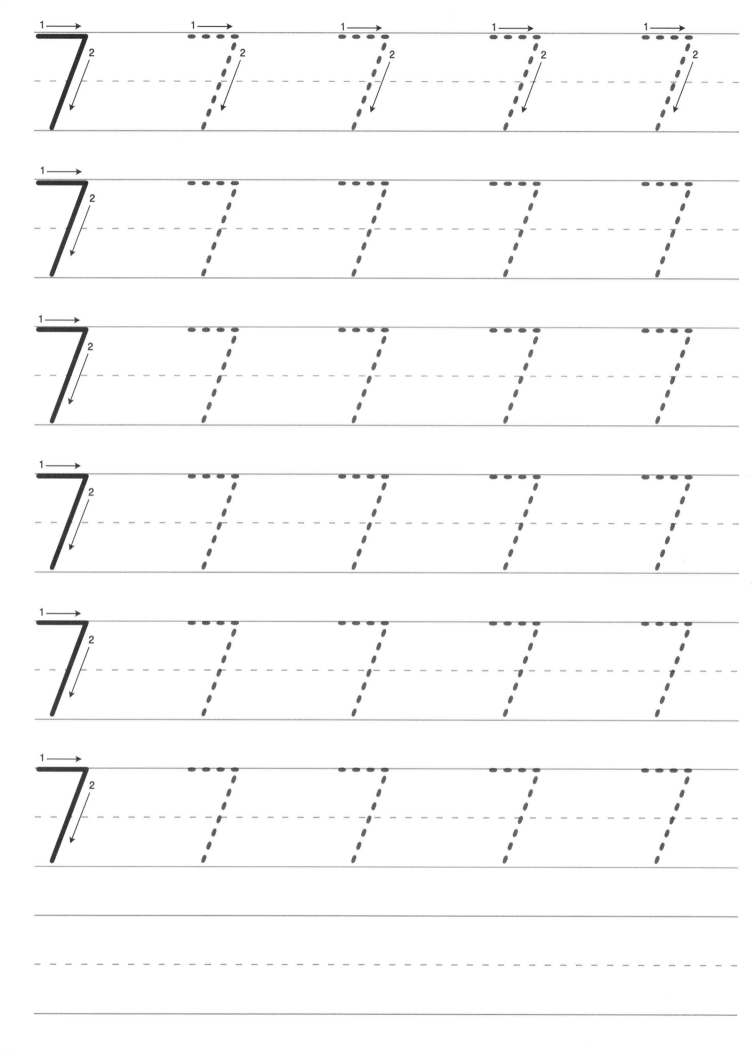

8 Eight Eggs

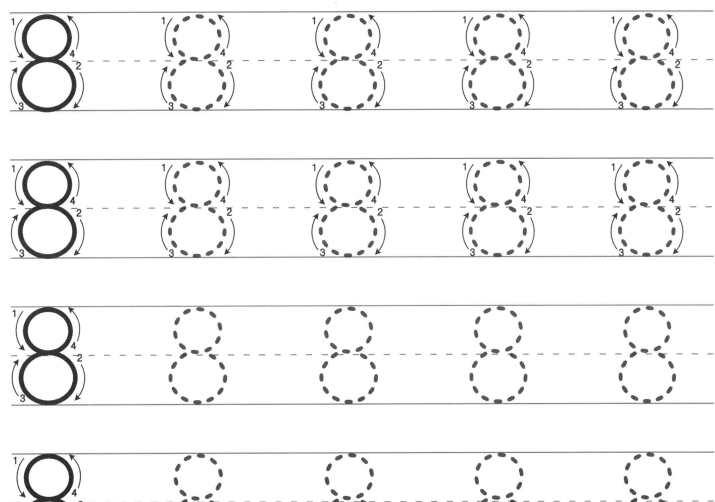

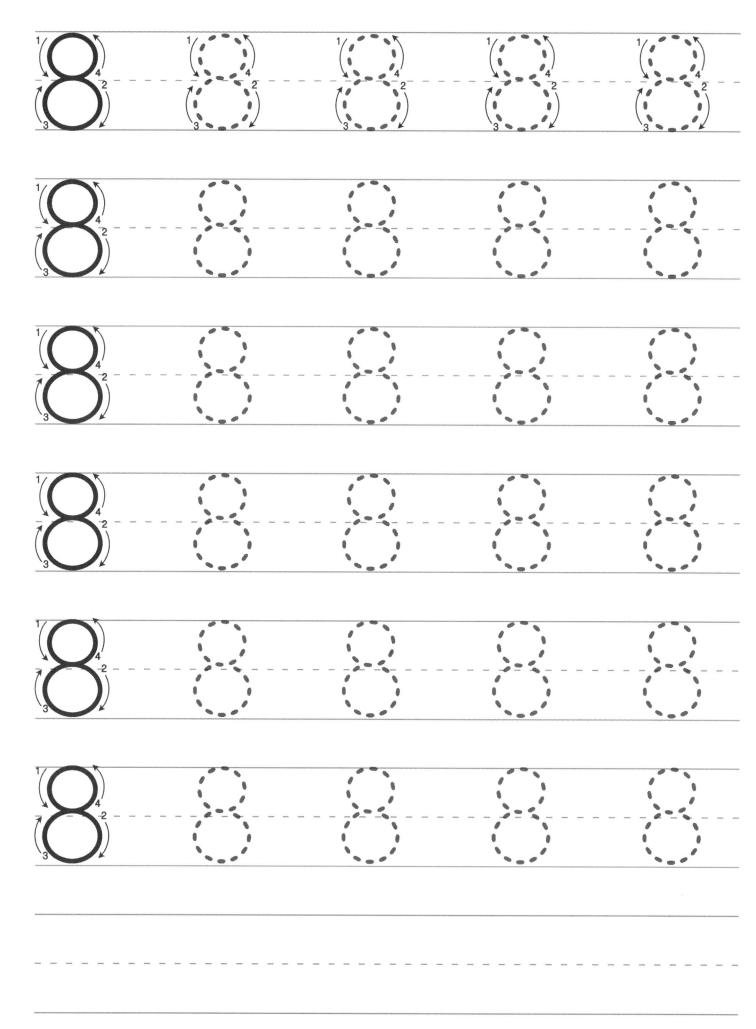

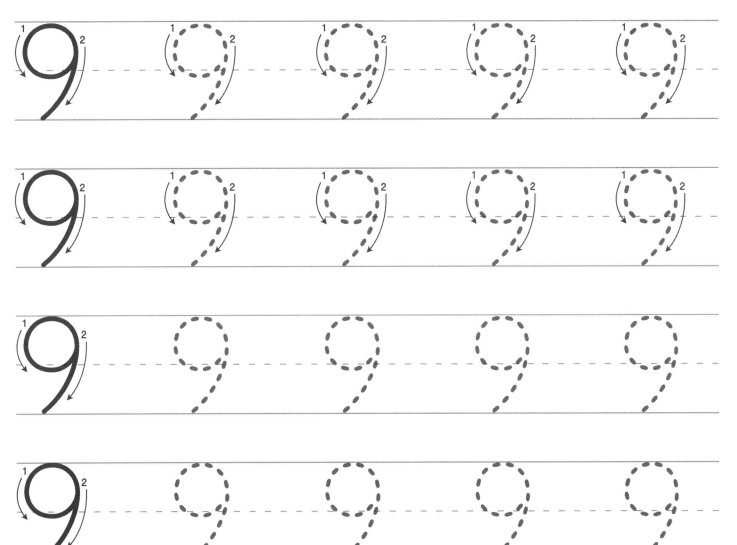

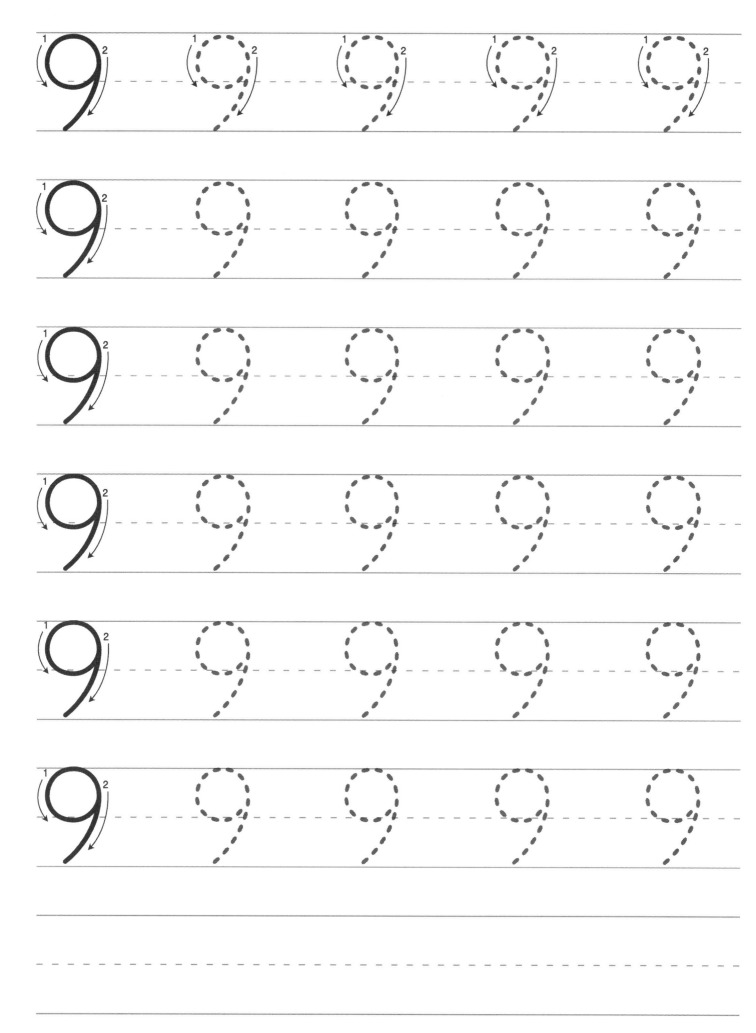

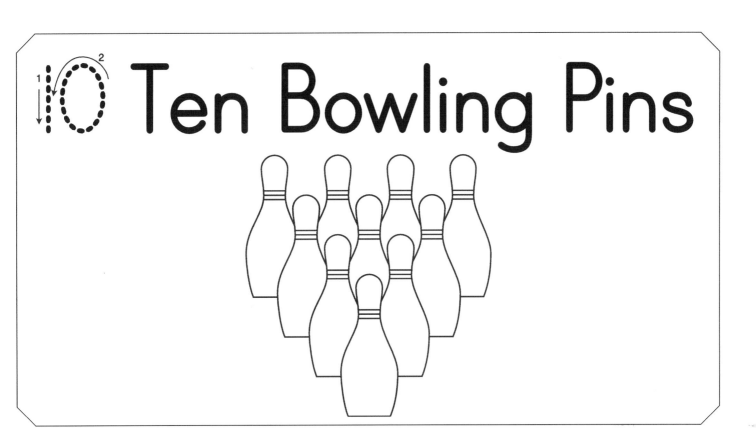

Ten Bowling Pins

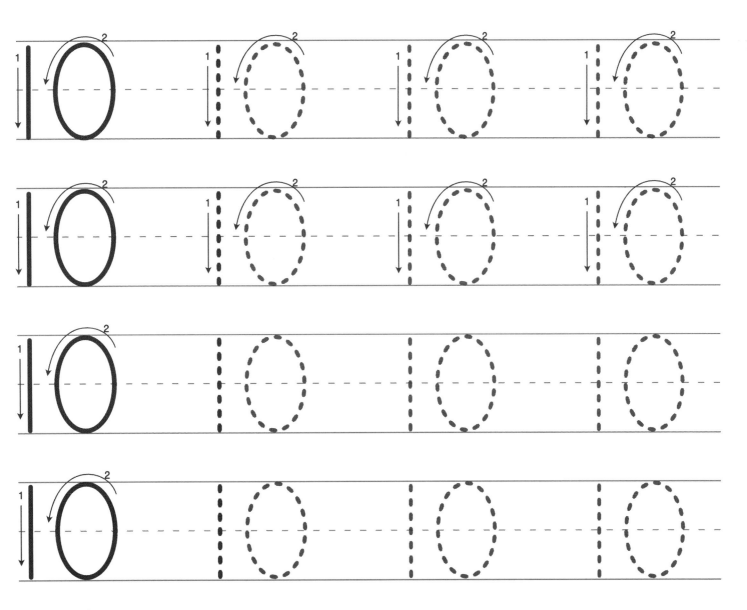

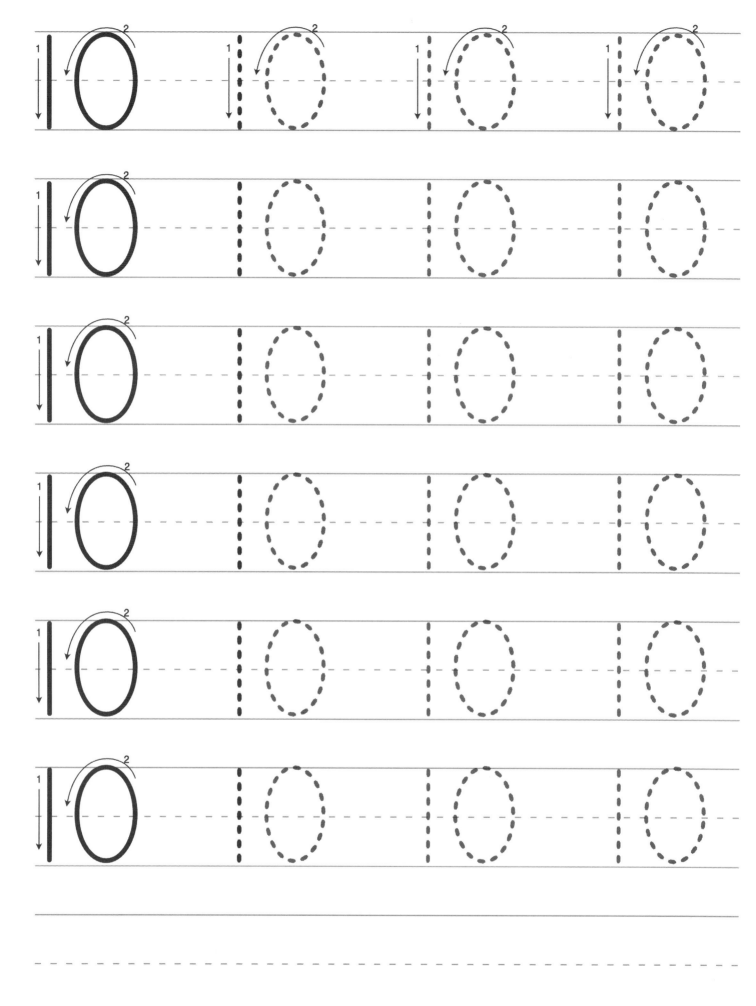

Made in United States
Orlando, FL
23 November 2021